MW00561303

Trading Systems

A new approach to system development and
portfolio optimisation

Emilio Tomasini & Urban Jaekle

HARRIMAN HOUSE LTD

3A Penns Road
Petersfield
Hampshire
GU32 2EW
GREAT BRITAIN

Tel: +44 (0)1730 233870
Fax: +44 (0)1730 233880
Email: enquiries@harriman-house.com
Website: www.harriman-house.com

First published in Great Britain in 2009 by Harriman House.

ISBN 978-1-905641-79-6

British Library Cataloguing in Publication Data
A CIP catalogue record for this book can be obtained from the British Library.

Printed in the UK by the Lightning Source

Contents

Emilio Tomasini:

To the loving memory of my mother Carla Ferrarini and of my father Ercole Tomasini

When days are dark and friends are few how I long for you

Urban Jaekle:

To my son Till and to my wife Inna

'If you want a guarantee, buy a toaster.'

Clint Eastwood

Acknowledgments

A special thank you to the publisher of *Traders* magazine, Lothar Albert, who allowed us to contribute to his valuable publication: without him we could not have understood that we too we have something important to say about trading systems' development. From those articles in *Traders* magazine and from the contacts with fellow traders that ensued we received an unparalleled intellectual enrichment.

Another warm thank you to Peter Müller and Bruno Stenger, publishers of TerminTrader.com. They invite us to their reputable conference about quantitative trading every March in Frankfurt: Urban and I met there for the first time and our professional relationship has withstood the passing of time.

Thanks to Dr. John Clayburg and to Pierre Orphelin, without them we would never have appreciated the importance of re-optimisation and walk forward analysis. And without the help of Leo Zamansky, CEO of RINA Systems, we would have never had the opportunity to work with Portfolio Maestro and had access to excellent assistance.

Thanks to Vittorio Pinelli, Giuseppe Lugli, Cristiano Raco, Antonio Giammaria, Thomas Wirth, Daniel Tydecks and Fabrizio Bocca for the precious contribution and support during recent years: they deserve credit for having helped us survive so far on the markets. And we can assure you that this is a not an easy task. A major part of this book derived from conversations and mutual help with them, and overall the major part of the research about equity line moving average crossovers and walk forward analysis is based on their contributions. Our final thanks go to Jeremy Davies and Evelina Pernicheva from TradeStation Europe. It is always a pleasure to meet them in London and to work together with them using their powerful software package and their brokerage expertise. All charts and data throughout this book – unless otherwise stated – are powered and created by TradeStation.

Preface

Our lives are deeply interlinked with trading systems. We have both been systematic traders since the 1990s and we can say we were only *lucky* to start this job when systematic trading and technical analysis were still considered by the academic world as being within the boundaries of fraudulent activity. You need to consider that we were born in an era where the tenet of the financial world was, at best, you cannot make money or at least not more money from the financial markets than from a properly optimised portfolio of assets.

This is false. Every day the sun rises on the horizon there are many traders that die and some of them that make a fortune. It happens seldom but it happens, as the names of William Eckhardt, Ed Seykota, Jim Simons, and many others remind us. And you can be one of them. We do not know if we are to be counted among those lucky quantitative traders, but we know that we have done it for so many years and we have met so many dead bodies of systematic traders that we can proudly state that luck cannot be the only driver of our survival.

Sometimes your experience will help you to understand what you are and where you are heading to. The story of this book started with this premise and it was developed to explain and demonstrate what a system developer should know and do in order to achieve success on the markets with trading systems. That is in short, to make money with a return higher than the majority of his fellow traders. We do not think that in order to build a winning trading system you need to be a rocket scientist; we are not rocket scientists ourselves. We are systematic traders that trade institutional money. We esteem that part of our survival is due to the meeting of other fellow traders and to the huge amount of research we have done over the years. If your research is a lonely trip, then your way to success must be a long one. We owe so much to other fellow traders, both from the retail market and from the institutional side of the market, that we felt it our duty to share our experience with all the traders that will buy this book.

Thanks to the frequent speeches we make in Frankfurt, London, Paris, Budapest and Milan we got in touch with quantitative traders from all around Europe, Asia and the US. These meetings were the driver of our success as traders. We hope this book will help you in finding your way among the uncharted waters of systematic trading as other books and other fortunate relationships with fellow traders helped us in achieving our trading success.

The book is divided into three parts. Part one is a short practical guide to trading systems' development and evaluation. This part, which is written by Emilio Tomasini, forms the theoretical basis for part two. It tries to condense our experience in a few practical tips that go beyond what you can find written in other books.

In part two, written by Urban Jaekle, readers will find a step-by-step development process that goes from the very initial code writing up to walk forward analysis and money management. This main part of the book was the result of the combination of Emilio Tomasini's experience and Urban Jaekle's practical application of trading systems and evaluation. We both put our ideas together in the programming work, system tests and evaluation of the presented methods.

Part three, written by Emilio Tomasini, treats the topic of portfolio composition: how to put all systems for all different markets together in the most effective way. We believe that this chapter regarding systematic portfolio composition is by far the most updated state of the art survey on how to build a portfolio. The book is completed with an appendix of systems and ideas from Urban Jaekle which we published within the last three years in about 20 different articles. Take it as a short basis to start building your own trading system portfolio with the help of the tools given to you within this book.

We remind readers, and also ourselves, that a trader can never say he achieved success but only that he survived: the black swan is always around the corner.

Please always keep in mind what the acclaimed trading systems' developer Thomas Stridsman writes:

> 'It is only a question of how long you stick around. If we all stick around long enough the probabilities have it that we all will be wiped out sooner or later. It is just a matter of time.'[1]

No piece of advice could be more appropriate for our book than this.

Good luck!

Emilio Tomasini tomasini@emiliotomasini.com

Urban Jaekle ujaekle@aol.com

---

[1] Stridsman, Thomas, *Trading Systems That Work,* (Wiley, 2001) [1].

Part I:

A Practical Guide to Trading System Development and Evaluation

1

What is a trading system?

Nowadays the term *trading system* conveys many meanings that can sometimes be misleading. A trading system is a precise set of rules that automatically defines, without any human discretionary intervention, the entry and the exit on the markets. Since rules are precise there is no doubt over when and where to apply them and this makes the trading system statistically testable. This means that we can figure out how the system performed in the past and how it could perform in the future with a certain degree of confidence. If you add a money management rule and a portfolio rule to the set of rules that define entry and exit on the market then you have a "trading strategy" or, in other terms, a completely automatic approach to the markets, given a starting capital.

When we talk about money management we are not talking about what is commonly believed to be risk management; that is, where to place an initial stop loss or a target price and so on. We are talking instead about "how much" to invest on a particular trade; that is, the position sizing or how many shares and how many futures contracts to buy and sell. And if we move to the construction of a portfolio of systems on uncorrelated price series, then money management is foremost what we should deal with in order to maximise the portfolio returns relative to the risk. Thus this process is also called portfolio management.

In more practical terms we can conclude that in order to develop and implement a trading system you need to have a software that easily performs all the programming and testing facilities and above all that goes directly to the market without any interference by the user. So we need to distinguish from a purely linguistic standpoint what a *trading system* is (or algorithmic trading) and what *automated trading* is. Indeed the latter could not exist without the first, but not vice versa. You could have algorithmic trading signals provided by a computer but not automatically place them on the markets. The main hindrance for the trading systems user is to produce trading signals that he is not mentally fit to place in the marketplace. To have a trading platform which automatically trades the mechanical signals produced by the trading system is thus a major advance.

1.1 An easy example of a trading system

So what does a trading system's pseudo code look like? It could be the following:

Buy 2 contracts at the highest high in the last 20 days;

Sell short 2 contracts at the lowest low in the last 20 days;

If marketposition = 1 then sell at last close – avgtruerange(14) stop;

If marketposition = -1 then buy to cover at last close + avgtruerange(14) stop.

We have an entry rule and we have a stop loss rule. This is a trading system. Its risk management is quite poor since we just wrote an initial stop loss which works also as a trailing stop, but the example is easy and quickly shows what a trading system is.

When the investor or the trader has a predefined set of rules that she or he applies discretionally in order to enter or exit the market, without any testing process and without any automation of the orders, and resting on a final judgment if and when to enter or exit the markets that could not be eventually classified ex ante, we could more appropriately talk of a "trading methodology". If the investor or the trader conducted detailed research on the past behaviour of the trading methodology, supporting it with statistical tests, and he has a disciplined character so that all the signals are equally placed on the market, we have something that is much closer to a trading system, without, in any case, being it. Since the "trading system" is much more precisely identified and it conveys an idea of a scientific work that underwent a strict statistical test, many investors or traders are tending to profess the use of a trading system instead of a trading methodology. A trading methodology always involves a bit of judgment and discretion.

Recently the financial industry has been swamped by the "quants", that is by money managers and traders that apply quantitative methods in order to produce buy and sell signals. What the difference is between a trading system and a quantitative forecasting method nobody knows, but since the term "quantitative finance" conveys an idea of something which is rigorously scientific and surely beyond the retail-oriented trumpery wares of common technical analysis, expect to meet many system traders that resell themselves as "quantitative traders". If the term "quantitative finance" serves to divide the system traders that base their decisions on statistics from those analysts that just grasp the artistic and esoteric side of technical analysis, we all agree on calling ourselves "quantitative traders".

Since a scientific appeal is the best way to sell something, there is nowadays a wide rush in the markets to give a deep scientific status to the trading systems industry. This approach seems to take for granted that a trading system must be a long series of rules, programmed in a complicated way, and full of breathtaking algorithms. Salesmen know very well that complexity raises prices. But it also raises the probability that a trading system will fail in the real world, and there is no approach more false than this.

Many commercially available formulas you can find in any technical analysis software, when properly tested and applied to price series, show a real market bias; that is they have a trustful predictive power. Trading systems could be very easy in their logical implementation, like a channel breakout, an indicator, a moving average, and to rely on your own trading decisions on something that is "easy" will not reduce your success probability; on the contrary it will increase it. On the way to success a lot will be done by money management and portfolio construction, risk management and timeframe, so do not be worried when you examine a trading formula that is simple and produces an equity line that appears unexciting, because you need to always reason under the portfolio constraint. It must be clear from the very beginning that a mediocre trading system – if applied to a portfolio of markets – will easily produce a good looking equity line.

1.2 Why you need a trading system

A huge economic literature shows without any doubt that just a few percent of traders are able to beat the market year after year. Most of both the retail and institutional traders sooner or later will go bust. If you do not belong to the lucky category of winning discretionary traders, then the only option for you in order to survive is the use of trading systems. If you have purchased this book you are most likely not a successful discretionary trader: in my experience successful discretionary traders are intuitively blessed and are unconsciously able to predict the market moves with their gut feeling. On the contrary there are many successful money managers, institutional and retail traders that profit from predetermined trading strategies and investing methodologies. But it would be misleading to think that a trading system could easily overcome all the hindrances trading creates. A trading system from one side could help the trader to beat the market but from the other side will create a new set of problems that a discretionary trader does not know.

First of all, if the trader has problems in terms of physical courage and some difficulties in pulling the trigger, trading systems will not be the ultimate solution. Like Larry Williams says, 'trading systems work, system traders do not'. There is no bigger infamy for a systematic trader than not to take a signal, as Bill Eckhardt wrote:

> *If you make a bad trade, you have money management, you have a whole bunch of things that will come to your aid, and you're really not in so much trouble if you make a bad trade. But if you miss a good trade there's really nowhere to turn. If you miss good trades with any regularity you're finished, you're doomed in this game.*

Second, in order to trust a trading system, especially during gloom periods when drawdown will erase the trader's confidence in the trading system's capabilities, you really need to do a huge amount of research and statistical work that not everybody is able to do. To develop, implement, test and evaluate a trading system is not an everyday job.

Finally, many of the drawbacks that affect discretionary trading still affect systematic trading, e.g. lack of sufficient starting capital, possibility to diversify the portfolio, full-time, 24-hour, dedication.

More importantly we can say that trading is not a rational enterprise, it is not an activity where you can, given some premises, arrive at a unique conclusion or where everything could be explained in a logical way. Fear and greed manipulate prices in a way that the human mind is unable to grasp. There are of course some fortunate discretionary traders that can beat the market with gut feeling but in these instances they do not often manage to fully explain why they buy or sell. If all this is true the consequence would be that you need a tool that is not rational and not logical to enter and exit the market, something that you could not fully understand, something that is counterintuitive. Usually the signals that you believe to be illogical or simply prone to failure will be the big winners.

To use a mechanical trading system means that you need to discard widely held beliefs about finance and over all discard the "feel-good" approach to trading: everybody usually feels comfortable buying dips and uncomfortable buying the highest high, but it may be the case that just the latter methodology is the good one. Testing a trading system could mean being forced by the brutal power of numbers to a trading attitude where you do not feel at ease. To be a fully mechanical trader means, in conclusion, to use violence against yourself. This is the only way to profits, unless you are one of the fortunate gun slingers that make money day after day and do not even know how.

1.3 The science of trading systems

It would be inappropriate to mix all the kinds and breeds of technical analysis available nowadays. There is a broad distinction between subjective and objective technical analysis.

> Objective technical analysis methods are well-defined repeatable procedures that issue unambiguous signals. This allows them to be implemented as computerised algorithms and back tested on historical data. Results produced by a back-test can be evaluated in a rigorous quantitative manner. Subjective technical analysis methods are not well-defined analysis procedures. Because of their vagueness, an analyst's private interpretations are required. This thwarts computerisation, back testing, and objective performance evaluation. In other words, it is impossible to either confirm or deny a subjective method's efficacy. For this reason they are insulated from evidentiary challenge.[2]

Subjective technical analysis did not gain a good reputation among the academic community or among serious market practitioners because of its vagueness and lack of scientific method. To be a chartist or a technical analyst, instead of a portfolio manager, using hidden technical analysis could be the least promising career launching pad in the financial industry. There is a wide sociological and psychological literature about why people believe weird things such as dogma, faith, myth and anecdotes so that it is much easier to isolate good scientific technical analysis using the approach of the scientific method. Without the intention to lecture here about philosophy of science we need to briefly remind readers what scientific knowledge is. Scientific knowledge is empirical or it is based on observations of reality:

> *'The essence of technical analysis is statistical inference. It attempts to discover generalisations from historical data in the form of patterns, rules and so forth and then extrapolate them to the future.'*[2]

So technical analysis, utilising the tools of statistical inference, starts from a sample of observations in order to gauge some statistical properties of the whole population. In this way technical analysis, like statistics, is quantitative. Further, technical analysis, like science, tries to predict the future through functional relationships among variables. If this variable does this then the dependent variable will do that. What in technical analysis is a rule in statistics is a functional relationship, which a certain probability is attached to. There is no barrier between scientific technical analysis and statistics so that all the doubts raised by those that dislike subjective technical analysis suddenly disappear. Quantitative technical analysis uses the typical method of analysis in applied sciences: the hypothetic-deductive method initiated by Newton and made famous by Popper. The hypothetic-deductive method has five stages [2]:

1. *Observation*. The system developer, through the continuous observation of the daily and intraday activity of the financial markets, devises a relationship among variables, i.e. among the daily volume activity and the closing price, or among the value of an indicator and the next day opening.

2. *Hypothesis*. This comes from the innovative mind of the system developer – an intellectual spark, the origins of which nobody knows. The system developer understands that the relationship he hypothesises is not due by chance to the particular nature of the sample he analysed, but it is common to the majority of the samples he can deduct from the whole population of data.

3. *Prediction*. If the relationship is true then a conditional proposition or a prediction can be constructed and 'the prediction tells us what should be observed in a new set of observations if the hypothesis is indeed true'[2].

4. *Verification*. The system developer verifies if the prediction holds true in a new set of observations.

5. *Conclusion*. The system developer, through the use of statistical inference tools such as confidence intervals and hypothesis tests, will decide if the hypothesis is true or false weighing whether new observations will confirm the predictions.

This process is in no way different from the scientific appraisal method used in applied sciences like chemistry or biology.

---

[2] Aronson, David, *Evidence-Based Technical Analysis*, Wiley, 2006, see [2].

2

Design, test, optimisation and evaluation of a trading system

2.1 Design

A trading system starts from an idea like an entrepreneurial vision. Innovation is something that lies in between creativity and fancy, and it can come independently from how much time you are dedicating to it. There are system traders that say that a good trading system idea comes when you are least expecting it, but conversations with good traders could help and it is highly recommended you attend seminars, congresses and friendly meetings among professional traders. Even watching discretionary traders at work can be useful. Unfortunately there is no sure path for innovation but the following tips can prompt you to walk beyond the boundaries of imagination.

Getting started

A good place to begin is the existing literature on algorithmic trading: you can take the bibliography of this book as a starting point.

Another serious source of good trading ideas is the technical specialised press including, among others:

1. *Traders* www.traders-mag.co.uk

2. *Active Trader* www.activetradermag.com

3. *Futures* www.futuresmag.com

4.   *The Technical Analyst* www.technicalanalyst.co.uk

5.   *Technical Analysis of Stocks & Commodities* www.traders.com

The forums of TradeStation deserve a particular mention. They are restricted to customers, but full of good free trading codes and ideas. Other trading platforms and their forums also provide valuable information and system development ideas.

On eMule you will find free information, including trading codes and sometimes pieces of software. In the past Omega Research, the software house producing TradeStation, issued a series of periodic papers called "System Traders and Development Club" (STAD) in which the TradeStation programmers took a code and dissected it, explaining how the code was built and showing all the programming tricks involved. This is the best place to start and you can find these old PDFs still circulating in traders' networks. At the time of writing, TradeStation plans to launch a 21st century version of the popular Strategy Trading and Development Club, which will be called TradeStation Labs. This online offering will deliver both free and premium content highlighting TradeStation's capabilities for unique custom technical and fundamental analysis and its practical uses for trading stocks, options, futures and forex.

The programming task

Usually beginners are scared when they are faced with the necessity of learning to program in a language like Easy Language (TradeStation) or MetaStock. The jitters are apparently greater for programming than for learning a foreign language, even though nobody could explain how a foreign language differs from a programming language. This is perhaps due to the fact that programming sounds mathematical and logical while to speak a foreign language is something most people are more accustomed to, and it is an endeavour where in any case you can help yourself with gestures and mimics. As far as we are concerned the contrary is true and it is much more difficult to learn Russian as a foreign language, for example, than to learn to program in Easy Language.

A system is comprised of an entry formula, an exit formula and a money management formula. The exit formula is concerned with "risk management", that is initial stop loss, trailing stop, target exit and generally how much money we risk and in which way we risk it in every trade. "Money management" is concerned with how much we invest on every trade, that is how many stocks or futures contracts we buy or sell. What beginner system traders tend not to trust is that returns will be astonishing only through an extensive and aggressive use of leverage and money management techniques or, put in another way, not even breath-taking trading systems can become viable investment tools if appropriate money and risk management tools are not applied.

Which timeframe to trade?

Usually retail traders are inclined to trade intraday because they think risks are lower while institutional traders could not usually endure the effort to watch the markets for 24 hours per day.

Nowadays it would be obsolete to consider just daytime trading sessions since most futures contracts are traded on the Globex market 24 hours a day. Even though major price moves still often happen during the US daylight trading sessions, if you project into the future what has happened so far and how fast globalisation has shaped financial markets, we anticipate that in the future there will be increasingly no difference between trading in the morning or during the night since shocks and counter shocks will affect the markets 24 hours per day. Liquidity is really changing the markets' behaviour, moving from one part of the world to another without any difficulty, and it is not rare today to meet US traders that trade German DAX futures. This is something that was absolutely impossible even to think about just 5 years ago, and if you think ahead in this direction you will recognise that it is impossible now to even mull over what the markets will be like in the next 10 years.

As far as our experience is concerned, trading today must be done 24 hours per day. There is no difference between intraday and daily approaches since there are so many liquid contracts around. Risks can be controlled choosing those markets and contracts where systems are efficient and stop losses will not destroy the initial capital even in the most unfortunate of the starts. Trading intraday, even with a platform that automatically places trades and stop losses like TradeStation, is a very demanding task and it is not compatible with any other work. Those thinking of the intraday business will be better off if they combine with a team of at least three fellow traders with whom to share the burden to follow markets 24 hours per day. Life is full of unexpected woes and to approach intraday systematic trading without a panel of strategies applied by a team of at least three traders is pure suicide.

Trading a daily timeframe is a more relaxing enterprise than intraday trading and can be approached even by those traders that have another daylight occupation. Discipline to place every day orders in the morning or at midday and checking positions as many times during the day as possible is very important. The biggest side effects of this approach –

drawdown and risk – can be levelled out with the choice of the most suitable futures contracts in terms of margin, volatility and liquidity. Trading intraday exposes the traders to huge unexpected price movements, energy blackout and platform inefficiencies. Conversely, trading a daily price series will raise the drawdown by a monetary absolute amount and it will also enlarge the flat equity line period. But nowadays traders have so many possibilities around the world that every account will find its appropriate futures margins and price volatility.

2.2 Test

The importance of the market data

The testing process is particularly difficult since the first problem a trader encounters is the market data. Today the access to market data is cheap and easy but notwithstanding a trader must apply great care in deciding the trustworthiness of the data. If 10 years ago data accuracy was a sheer nightmare for the serious trader, today the facility with which they can be retrieved often overlooks drawbacks almost every data vendor has. For example, there are data vendors that for unknown reasons consider the closing price to be something different from the last traded price and, if your trading algorithm uses the closing price as a filter, test results will consequently be different from what you expect.

Other data vendors provide open prices systematically different from the real ones, usually when the opening price is the result of an auction that takes place before continuous trading begins, and some data vendors have different daily highest high or daily lowest lows. They can also get confused when the trading session is different from the ordinary one, as is the case with CME futures on Sundays, when the trading session starts one hour earlier than usual during the week. So, even if everything looks simple, a systematic trader should always pay great attention to the accuracy of the price data, and it is a worthwhile exercise to compare the price series of one data vendor with the price series of a different one in order to understand what will happen when applying the system with real money.

The most commonly used daily data source by traders are CSI data (www.csidata.com) and Pinnacle data (www.pinnacledata.com).

When you are considering stock prices there is nothing trickier overall than if you go on the long run. In the long run stock prices will inevitably be fallacious because a company may sooner or later merge with another one, it may change its core business, undergo a corporate split, or the company may simply go bust and be delisted. For example, the acquisition of Mannesmann by British Vodafone in 1999, where the takeover doubled Vodafone's value and changed its company structure. Another example is the merger of AOL and Time Warner in the US.

So when you apply a system on a 40-year stock price series you really need to wonder what you are trading. This is the major drawback in relation to which other difficulties – such as the dividend policy – can be easily dealt with. Obviously the gap due to dividend payment must be taken into consideration and price series accordingly rectified, a task that is performed, more or less promptly, by every serious data vendor.

Futures price series do not have any lesser problems: futures last from one month (like, for example, futures on energy products like NYMEX Crude Oil) up to 14 months (like, for example, on cereal futures markets) so that if you want to apply a system to a 50-year grain price series you will have the problem of connecting one expiration date to the following one. Usually literature about futures relies on three major methods:

1. Same expiration contracts

The individual contracts are connected according to the expiration months. That is, for example, you connect September Corn 2001 with September Corn 2002 and September Corn 2003 and so on. This approach is possible where every single expiration month goes close to its peer forthcoming expiration month, the closer the better, and it is best when it overlaps the forthcoming contract by some months as in the case with cereal markets. Surely this approach is not possible on a stock index that usually lasts three months or on an energy futures index that usually lasts one month.

On commodities that have a seasonal stocking industry that brings the unconsumed production on a given year to the following one, prices tend to assume a similar pattern according to the expiration months. With US corn, for example, which is harvested from September to October, the same players are involved (farmers, stocking industry entrepreneurs, cattle breeders, etc) on the September expiration contract each year and so they tend to assume the same behavioural pattern. In other terms it is more proper to create a price series with all the September expiration months connected together than a continuous or perpetual price series that mixes up different delivery months that have nothing in common.

2. Continuous contracts

The continuous contract is an artificial "collage" of the different forthcoming delivery months. The rationale of the continuous contract is that the forthcoming contract is the most liquid and the most traded so that if you add up all the forthcoming contracts you will have a significant price series. The problem is that on the delivery day you will have a gap between the old expiration month and the new one. This gap is what happens in reality when you are trading real money. If you are in a trade and you need to switch to the successive contract before the delivery day of the expiration contract you will add up or subtract the difference in prices on the expiration day from the eventual result of the trade.

3. Perpetual contracts

In order to avoid the above mentioned hurdle from the price gap on the expiration day the perpetual contract was created. This is a mathematical representation of the past data series where the old prices are updated according to the gap in the last expiration day. On the "point-based" update the difference in absolute terms is subtracted or added from the whole price series, on the "ratio-adjusted" price series it is usually subtracted from or added to a percentage equal to the price gap. In this way the relative difference in historical price swings is kept constant. More complex methods for perpetual contracts exist but they go beyond the scope of this paragraph [1]. The ultimate result of a perpetual price series is that it is not a real one and the more extrapolated the more you are applying a system to something that is far from reality.

The length of your back-testing period

Literature points to the fact that a trading system, in order to be robust and consistent, must be more or less successful on a multi-period multi-market test. This is an important point that, with the newest generation of computers, has been put under scrutiny thanks to the fast speed of making calculations and cheap availability of historical price series. According to some mechanical traders the multi-market rule should be limited since systems have their own personality that suits only a certain batch of markets but not all. Rare are the systems that can withstand the multi-market test in the sense that they work equally well on many different markets (bonds, equity, commodities, currencies, stocks, etc). We share the same opinion with these traders – after 20 years experience we can today count the real multi-market systems on the fingers of just one hand.

Conversely, as far as multi-period tests are concerned, other mechanical traders point to the fact that past is past: markets change continuously because economy, institutional structure and society change. So why expect markets to behave in the same way year after year? There are many system traders that for intraday trading systems will never test back more than 12 months and others will test back just 3 months. We will see shortly how optimisation and re-optimisation will fit into this whole picture. So far we can just express our point of view, which is neither permissive nor strictly rigid.

We think that the length of the back-testing period should be decided with some ordinary acumen derived from experience. For example, let's consider a banking stock that traditionally had a choppy price series. Suddenly this bank merges with an online bank during the 2000 bubble. In 2001 it would be inappropriate to test a system on the price series before the merger because it is something that has changed so abruptly. Another example is with euro/dollar. Many data providers offer customers a euro/dollar price series derived, or worse extrapolated, in some way before 2003. Other data vendors simply extrapolate the euro/dollar price series before 2003, making a proportion with the Deutsche mark/dollar pair. It is obvious that it would be fatal to test a system on a euro/dollar price series starting from 1960 (yes, there are data vendors that sell this dubious data) expecting with faith that it will perform the same in 2008. Or it would be inappropriate to test a system on a Bund data series when it was still traded on open outcry in London in the 1980s. It is also clear that a serious trader should cut away abnormal circumstances like the stock bubble in 1999-2000 or the crude oil spike in 2008. Every system works when volatility is huge and market movements are the widest. But only a robust and consistent system will always work in normal conditions. Abnormal conditions will happen and we know that we will face them. But markets will be normal 80% of the time and a good system knows when a market is really out of control and risks are too high.

Rule complexity and degrees of freedom

The first aim of a multi-market test is to check if a system performs in the way it is supposed to (that is signals, if checked manually, are in the same position the programmer wants) and if it is profitable on the average of the markets on which it was applied. We should not expect a system to be profitable on every market we test it with but the more markets the system tests positively with the better.

Testing serves the need to check the system's statistical validity at a first glance, while optimisation serves the need to fine-tune the system to the particular behavioural feature of a market. Although this is only a partial definition it helps to clarify that optimisation comes after testing – that is after we have decided the system is sound.

The usual result will be that a system performs profitably on similar contracts; that is, for example it will perform the same way on all the energy futures but worse on all the different bond contracts and moderately well on currencies.

The most important choice while testing a system is to decide the size of the test window; that is how much of the price series we need to apply the system to. This decision does not follow a clear-cut schedule or rule of thumb but it needs to respect two statistical requirements: the price series must be long enough to entail different market situations and to produce a significant number of trades.

The number of variables and the data they consume are also considered in relation to the whole data sample under an approach known as "degrees of freedom" – that is, the number of variables and conditions and the data they use should not be more than a 10% fraction of the whole data sample considered. It is of critical importance to avoid a situation where we have 500 trading days and a trading system with 500 different conditions. It could be that each condition is different from the remaining 499 and it only fits to that particular trading day, so that every day will have its own proper condition that will make the most money from the market in sample, but it will have no forecasting power (see Chapter 5).

Rule complexity and degrees of freedom are a hard topic for those not mathematically oriented. But even among mathematicians there are many that would not be at ease in explaining what degrees of freedom are. When explaining degrees of freedom (usually indicated as df) maybe the most appropriate and easy to grasp explanation is the joke of the married man that comments, 'There is only one subject, my wife, and my degree of freedom is zero. I should increase my "sample size" by looking at other women.'

Coming to a more serious approach we should say that there are many definitions of the concept "degrees of freedom" varying from statistics to mathematics, geometry, physics and mechanics. An interesting paper available free on the internet performs the difficult task of making the concept simple[3]. A first definition (Larry Toothaker, 1986) could be 'the number of independent components minus the number of estimated parameters'. This definition is based upon the Walker (1940) definition: 'The number of observations minus the number of necessary relations among these observations'. But the best practical way to explain the concept is an illustration introduced by Dr. Robert Schulle (University of Oklahoma):

In a scatter plot when there is only one data point, you cannot make any estimation of the regression line. The line can go in any direction … Here you have no degrees of freedom (n-1 = 0 where n = 1) for estimation (this may remind you of the joke about the married man). In order to plot a regression line you must have at least two data points (a wife and a mistress). In this case you have one degree of freedom for estimation (n-1 = 1 where n = 2). In other words, the degree of freedom tells you the number of useful data for estimation. However, when you have two data points only, you can always join them to be a straight regression line and get a perfect correlation (determination index = 1.00). Thus the lower the degree of freedom is, the poorer the estimation is.

So even in an intuitive way we arrive at the conclusion that the wider the sample size and the lower the number of variables, the better the estimation. Robert Pardo is the only author in the current literature that is able to keep the topic manageable and he gives the following short-cut guidelines in his book [4]:

```
Calculation of the degrees of freedom = whole data sample -
rules and conditions - data consumed by rules and conditions
```

Generally, less than 90% remaining degrees of freedom is considered too few. Beyond the Pardo's formulas that can help from a practical standpoint it is important to remember that a system with 20 variables cannot be tested on just 6 months of daily data in order to decide, if going ahead with a proper optimisation. The number of variables and conditions of the trading system are intimately connected to the length of the testing period. Put in another way, some estimates are based on more information than others. The number of degrees of freedom of an estimate is the number of independent pieces of information on which the estimate is based. The more information, the more accurate the estimate. The more information the higher the number of the degrees of freedom.

The same concept of the at least 90% degrees of freedom left could be applied in reverse as a rule of thumb with a multiple of 10 to the relationship between data used by the system's calculations and the testing window length. If you apply a 30-day moving average of the closing price you need to test it over at least 300 days (30 x 10).

Let's make one example: we consider a data sample of three years of highs, lows, opens and closing prices for a total 260 day per year x 3 x 4 = 3120 data points. We consider then a trading strategy uses a 20-day average of highs and a 60-day average of lows. The first average uses 21 degrees of freedom: 20 highs plus 1 more as a rule, and the second average uses 61 degrees of freedom: 60 lows plus 1 as a rule. The total is 82 degrees of freedom used in the example. The result in percentage terms is 82/3120 = 2.6% so that 97.4% degrees of freedom are left.

Data points used twice in calculations are counted once so that if you are using a 5-day moving average of the closes and a 10-day moving average of the closes you will have for the latter condition 10 data + 1 rule while for the first condition you will have just 1 rule. The total is 12 data consumed. It is obvious that since the 5-day moving average is included into the longer one only the latter will be relevant for the degrees of freedom calculations.

The number of trades required in order to trust a system is also connected to the length of the testing windows. A test is significant if it produces a number of trades that will allow the risk of being wrong to be kept at the lowest level. The test window's length should take care of this. Let's say that the obvious standard error should be added to or subtracted from all the trading system's report parameters according to the trade sample. Standard error is:

```
Standard Error = square root of n + 1

Where n = number of the trades
```

The higher the number of trades, the lower the possible error in the trading system's metrics. In other words if we have few trades, the risk that these trades are profitable by accident is high. If you shoot once and you hit the bull's-eye it is possible either that you are a good marksman or simply that you are lucky. Conversely if you shoot 100 times and you hit the mark every time the probabilities that you are a good marksman are higher.

To be considered trustworthy, a system needs at least 100 trades, so that its standard error will be the square root of 100 + 1 = + - 10.04%.

All the trading system metrics will vary in between the boundaries of +10% and - 10%. That is, if the net profit is $100 the possible real net profit will vary more or less as a rule of thumb from a high at $110 to a low at $90.

2.3 The forecasting power of a trading system

Optimisation

Optimisation has earned a bad reputation among many traders. It can even be an offense for a systematic trader. Optimising a system means to find those inputs in the system's variables that maximise profits or that fulfill whichever constraints a trader decides to be the leading criteria for optimisation (for instance instead of maximising profits a system could tend to minimise drawdown). Let us give an example: you have a moving average crossover system; that is, the system buys when the short-term moving average crosses the long-term moving average. The question optimisation replies to is how many days will be the input of the short-term moving average and how many days will be the input of the long-term moving average. Optimisation means "to make fit" a system; that is, to adapt a system to the market we intend to trade [4].

But optimisation is a two-edged sword: it is one thing to adapt a system to a market in terms of volatility, initial risk, return, etc. But it is another thing to look for those inputs that by chance made the most money in the past but have no forecasting power. Let's assume that we have a system that every day will buy at the lowest price and sell at the highest price with two inputs that will have the precise entry and exit price by which the maximum profit is reaped. This is a wrong kind of optimisation since we looked for a value that changes every day and only with hindsight is the best value for that particular day able to be defined. This system has no forecasting power.

It is absolutely impossible to avoid optimisation in trading systems' development. Just think of what every trader is currently doing and you will understand that optimisation is something we need to face. There are traders that refuse the inputs optimisation process since, according to their view, a system should work forever with the same inputs. But then they decide to trade a system among a batch of other systems simply because in the past it made more money than other systems. Isn't this a kind of optimisation? Again they change the original system code adding constraints and conditions in order to adjust the system to market price behaviour and then they chose the variation of the system that worked the best in the past: isn't this also a kind of optimisation? If you are currently not so much inclined towards optimisation please review your standpoint and consider how many times you have used optimisation involuntarily.

Optimisation is something useful in system trading and we need to distinguish between the normal optimisation process and its aberration, namely curve fitting or over-optimisation. For example: we trade a daily system on bond futures that will be consequently affected by monetary policy. Monetary policy is not something that changes every day but it suits the economic cycle of expansion-recession so that we are talking about something that lasts years. It will be clear in this case that we need to have an optimisation window that is 6, 12 or 18 months long – something of a reasonable length in order to fine-tune the system with the market and the monetary policy.

Provided the system produces a significant number of trades, we will test the system on the preceding two years at the beginning and then we will fine-tune the system, re-optimising it every 6, 12 or 18 months. This approach is directed toward real trading and not a theoretical appraisal of the system. Surely the system must be tested on the longest price series we have at our disposal and optimised accordingly in order to check at a first glance if the system is viable. But this process is not something that will help us in finding the appropriate parameters to place the next trades. It is simply an evaluation process that will help us in deciding if the system is suitable for that particular market; that is, if the equity line is growing (the equity line may not be growing in a smooth way as we would wish, but it should at least be decisively on the upside).

In other words during testing over the longest price series available we check if the system is adapted to catch the moves of a particular market, while during optimisation we see if there is room for improvement with a change of inputs. Then through periodic re-optimisation within a 6 to 12 month window we fine-tune the system, in terms of inputs, to the characteristics of that particular market and keep the system abreast of the market changes.

For an intraday system all the testing, optimising and re-optimising periods will be shorter than for daily or weekly systems.

Walk forward analysis

In conclusion we can state that optimisation is something variable in terms of data window since systems need to be kept in synchronisation with the market. Before computer power became so cheap and easy to employ for the majority of market players, an "out-of-sample period" was always recommended after optimisation by all the trading systems' developers. The "out-of-sample period" is a data window (usually 10 to 20% of the whole optimisation data window) we keep outside the optimisation process and which we apply to the optimised trading system in order to verify its forecasting power over unseen data. If the system performs in the same manner over the unseen data of the "out-of-sample data" it means that the system is a robust one and it can be traded with confidence.

So far we have only discussed ideas that you can read in any of the books in circulation about trading systems. But this is an obsolete view of optimisation, maybe dating back to those times where computer power was neither cheap nor widely available. Today optimisation has evolved into a more efficient and proper method of testing and making a system fit over a long price series. This method goes under the name of "walk forward analysis" or "walk forward testing".

Walk forward testing is a kind of multiple and successive out-of-sample test over the same data series. Let us give an example: a system is optimised over the first two years of the data history and then applied over the subsequent 6 months of unseen data. Then the optimisation window moves ahead by a 6-month period and a new optimisation takes place in order to find the new inputs that will be applied over the forthcoming 6 months of data. And so on. This kind of optimisation is a "rolling" walk forward analysis since the starting period of the optimisation window is always moving ahead by a 6-month period each time we re-optimise the inputs. If the starting period is always the same and the optimisation period gets longer and longer as the time goes by we have an "anchored" walk forward analysis. For intraday systems the "rolling" walk forward analysis is more appropriate since intraday trading systems are more suited to the changing market conditions.

Figure 2.1: A graphical description of a "rolling" and "anchored" walk forward analysis

---

Rolling walk forward: out-of-sample (OOS) = 20%:

Run #1 |--------- In-sample 80% -------------- | OOS 20% |

Run #2 |---------- In-sample 80% ------------| OOS 20% |

Run #3 |---------- In-sample 80% --------------------| OOS 20% |

Anchored walk forward: out-of-sample (OOS) = 20%:

Run #1 |--------------In-sample 80% --------------- | OOS 20% |

Run #2 |--------------------------- In-sample 80% ---------------| OOS 20% |

Run #3 |--- In-sample 80% --------------- | OOS 20% |

The equity line resulting from a walk forward run is where we are closest to reality in trading systems development since it is what real trading will produce in our pockets. And with no surprise this walk forward analysis equity line will be deeply different from the equity line we can produce with testing and optimising a trading system on the whole price series. So often traders fool themselves deciding whether a trading system is to be discarded or not based on a whole price series equity line that in reality reveals nothing about the real trading situation after periodic re-optimisation.

A widely accepted way to gauge the forecasting power of a system and its consistency is to calculate the ratio between the annualised net profit relating to the walk forward tests and the annualised net profit reaped during the optimisation periods. This is the walk forward efficiency ratio. If the ratio is above the 100% threshold then the system is efficient and the probability that it will keep its forecasting power during real trading is high. If a trader decides to trade a system with a walk forward efficiency ratio of just 50% (and many traders accept this level as the lowest possible) they should expect a system that performs at least at half the level of the performances indicated into the optimisation test. Statistical evidence also pinpoints that a poorly optimised system could make good performances on some lucky one or two walk forward tests. To avoid this trap the highest possible number of tests should be performed or at least 10 walk forward analysis tests with a test window (that is the data window where we apply the optimised trading systems) of at least 10 to 20% of the whole optimisation price series.

Every comment on the old type of static "out-of-sample" testing on the last part of the price series or on how to optimise a trading system is nowadays obsolete since most professional trading system development software has a walk forward analysis feature (like for example most of the RINA Systems products and in particular Portfolio Maestro). This does not mean that traders should not become accustomed to the ordinary testing and optimisation process. We recommend before using WFA you should do the ordinary homework about optimisation in order to acquire a full view of the system and its performances. To run a full walk forward analysis takes much time, so it is quicker to check the robustness of the system with a shift test and then another shift optimisation. In any case, for the sake of simplicity we will summarise some good tips about optimisation.

If we have many inputs to be optimised the best methodology is to test one or two inputs per turn while all other inputs are kept static. In this way the risk of over-optimisation is kept at the lowest level since it is impossible to find the batch of inputs that will maximise the constraint we gave to the equation simply because the inputs will not be optimised together in the same run.

Robustness

But can we deduce from the post-optimisation window if the system is robust or whether it is the product of over-optimisation? We do not need to trust the area of the best performing inputs as a sure way to victory. If enough darts are thrown at the board, a high-scoring grouping will occur or, put in another manner, if a monkey is put in front of a piano and enough time is allotted, it will eventually compose a sonata. This joke suggests that, at very least, the average of the results should be profitable if we want to trust the most performing inputs. If just 1 to 5% of the results are profitable this could have happened by accident: if the system's variables are given wide enough input ranges eventually the system will make a fortune over the past data. A robust system will show post-optimisation positive performances not only in 5% of all the tests but on the average of the tests. In other words, if the average results are positive then we can assume that the trading system is a robust one. If you are more statistically inclined you can also subtract the standard deviation (or a multiple of it) from the average net profit and check if the average net profit remains positive in this case.

So the number of inputs, conditions and variables must be kept under control and reduced to its minimum term. But how many inputs, conditions and variables are too many? This is a controversial area where the unique hallmark is the number of degrees of freedom that must always respect the numerical condition we depicted in the previous paragraph. Before taking an input into consideration it is obviously important to check with a rapid and cursory optimisation if the input varies or if it does not have any change under optimisation. If not, keep it constant in order to increase the degrees of freedom.

Another point to be considered is what scan range to choose for each input. An example will give a clearer picture of this problem: if you want to test a moving average crossover system with a short-term moving average and a long-term moving average on daily data, you cannot test the short moving average from 1 to 20 (this is what is considered the short term with daily data) and the long moving average from 20 to 200 (the latter is the interval that is usually considered long term with daily data). Indeed a step from 1 to 2 is a 100% change and a step from 19 to 20 is a 5% change. But a step change from 199 to 200 is just a 0.5 % change. You need to put the step scan range in an almost parallel relationship so that the scan from 1 to 20 will be performed with a step of 2 and the scan from 20 to 200 will be performed with a step of 20.

After optimisation is done a critical decision should be taken: which inputs' batch should we choose? First of all what we need to do is create a function chart that puts the variable's inputs scan range in relation to the net profits (or whichever else criteria was chosen for optimisation).

Figure 2.2: In the middle of the chart as the variable varies the net profit stays almost at the same level.

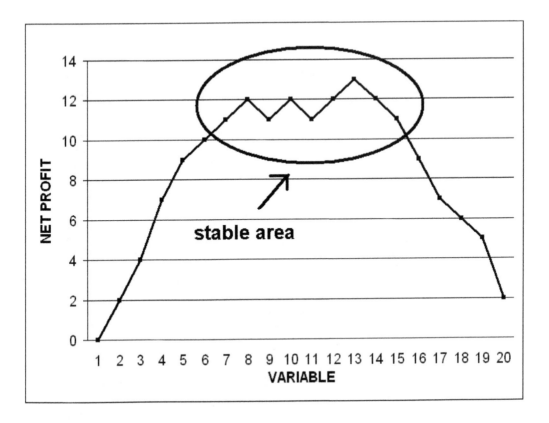

What we are looking for is a line that ideally would be as close as possible to a horizontal line, so that the net profit is not dependent on the input values. Reality is much different from theory so that we should be content with a line that grows lightly, then tops for a while and then decreases. The topping level is what we are looking for, that is an area where, even when changing the inputs, the net profits stay almost constant. This is the area where the robust input values are. This is diametrically opposite to a profit spike, that is a point in the line where net profit is high but it decreases deeply in the surrounding values. In other words we need to find an area where even after changing the input values net profit stays stable.

Figure 2.3: As much as the variable changes the net profit shows deep and wide swings: there is no area where at the variable's changing net profit stays more or less stable.

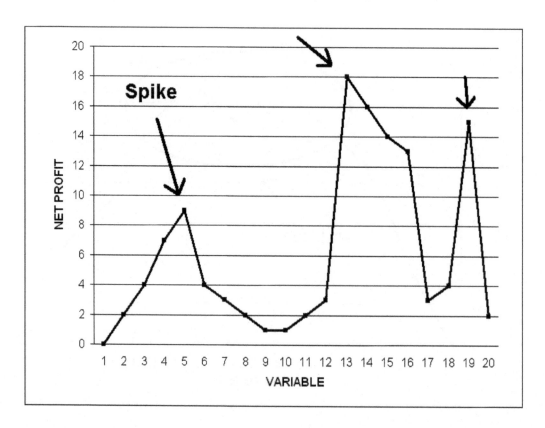

In summary we can state that there should be a logical path into the inputs' results so that something coherent in terms of inputs' batch should arise. When there is not a linear relationship with inputs and net profits, or drawdown, or whichever constraint you are putting as a primary rule of the optimisation, the whole set of results must be regarded as suspicious.

2.4 Evaluation of a trading system

Evaluating a trading system can look easier than it is in reality. In the end what a prudent trader must do is something which is counterintuitive: at first glance we indeed would say that the higher the net profit the better the system. Unfortunately nothing is further from reality than this impression. We will put forward some general methodological criteria not based on net profit and absolute numbers in order to weed out this deceptive approach. Then we will introduce the indicator RINA index, which was elaborated by TradeStation. RINA index is more and more common among system traders and we believe that it comes closer to a good analysis than any other tool.

What to look for in an indicator

Net profit is how much money the system brought home during the testing period. Even if the absolute number can lure the reader, it fundamentally says nothing about real performances of the system and moreover it says nothing about risk. Talking about profit without quantifying risk is a fatal error in system analysis. Furthermore, if you add proper commissions and slippage the equity line shape could change up to the point it becomes downward sloping or indeed negative.

So the two starting general considerations are the following:

1. A versatile return indicator should be normalised so that it can be easily comparable among multiple asset classes or multiple trading systems

2. A prudent indicator always compares return to risk

Net profit has neither of these features.

Moreover an indicator should always convey the idea of how much the measure he is trying to catch is "consistent". What is consistency? A synonym of consistency could be "stability": consistency measures how stable an indicator is. Let's take the example of the net profit: net profit in itself says nothing about "when" the profit was reaped. It could be that profit varied a lot from year to year or even that it was made just in a single year and all the other years the system lost money. Would you place more trust in a system that makes money year after year or simply a system that made money 10 years ago and then lost money every year since? In the end this later system made money because the profit was so huge 10 years ago and the following losses were acceptable; but who would be able to follow this system in the future? Nobody will trade such a system because it is apparent that the windfall 10 years ago could likely be an outlier, an abnormal occurrence that will never be repeated.

So we can conclude that a consistent trading system has an even distribution not only of profits and losses but also of the series of consecutive winning and losing trades. If you cut the statistics of a consistent trading system year by year you will find all the indicators will be almost the same. If substantial differences arise from year to year or from month to month the trading system is not consistent. An intraday system could also be gauged by weekly performances.

Average trade

An important indicator of the goodness of a trading system is the *average trade*, that is the net profit divided by the number of trades. Average trade tells us how much money we make or lose per trade. In absolute terms the average trade should be capable of covering slippage and commissions and then still leave some profit for the trader. In percentage terms the average trade should be consistent throughout the whole testing period. Usually traders compare the absolute average trade with the entry price of that particular trade so that it is expressed in percentage terms. Other traders compare the nominal average trade value with the nominal value of the contract in a given period. What we can recommend is to plot the historical average percentage value of the trades in order to have a clear picture of the profitability trend of the system over the years.

Percentage of profitable trades

The *percent profitable trades* number expresses the number of winning trades out of the number of the total trades. It is important not by itself (a trend following system can have a low percent profitable trades number such as 35% and still be a viable system) but because it can be used to gauge how the system is balanced in relation to the average winning trade/average losing trade ratio. Usually the logic is that if you win a lot of times the average winning trade/average losing trade ratio will be low, while if conversely your percentage of profitable trades is low then the ratio will be high (inverse relationship). A 50% percent profitable trades number is a healthy one. If it grows significantly over 50% (for example to 60% or 70%) be watchful because something could be wrong: to counterbalance such a high percentage the average winning trade/average losing trade ratio should be particularly low, often even under the alarm level of 1. If you are using target exit (let's assume you exit 50% of the position at a price limit over the entry) it is normal for the percentage of profitable trades to go over 60% and the average winning trade/average losing trade to go under 2.

The percentage of profitable trades number is also important for calculating the mathematical expectancy of a trading system. The percentage of profitable trades multiplied by the average winning trade should be higher than the percentage of losing trades multiplied by the average losing trade. Mathematical expectancy, in other words, should be positive and the higher the better. You can use this measure of mathematical expectancy to rank systems and pick up the best.

As far as the percentage of profitable trades is concerned there is a caveat that must be regarded with careful attention: a 50% profitable trades ratio does not mean that a loss is followed by a win or vice versa. It is a controversial area if a trade sequence suggests it is possible to claim that a win follows a win or vice versa in some order. Even if the topic is fascinating, a prudent trade should always fight against the worst and hope for the best so that in our experience to trust on trade dependency is particularly risky since the assumption is quite strong. Indeed you are assuming that there is a recurring order in the trade sequence; that is, probabilities in the past show that after three wins in a row it was more likely to have two losses instead of a fourth win.

There are roulette players which really believe that the chance of getting a red number in the next run increases if you just had a black one. And even worse, they believe that the chance of getting a red number becomes bigger and bigger if a row of subsequent black numbers occurs, for example 7 or 10 times in a row. From logical thinking and statistical theory, however, you know that each run of the roulette in the casino is completely independent from another. So it has no meaning, neither good nor bad, if in the run just before there was a red number, a black one or the green one. Each occurrence of a number is completely independent from the other ones. So betting on a colour in the next run your chance is always the same: $18/37 = 48.6\%$ (since there are 18 black and 18 red numbers plus one green 0).

Although the financial markets, especially for beginners, sometimes look like a casino, they are very different and more complex. In many cases they behave accidentally, with many movements happening up and down and nobody knows why. There are however some special situations which are created by human psychology of greed and fear when the market behaves differently to accident. It is these movements where, in special trading systems in special situations, trade dependencies can occur [5]. But this is a sophisticated topic that goes beyond of the scope of this book. In any case we recommend readers approach this topic with extreme prudence.

Profit factor

Profit factor is a perfect indicator for comparing different systems or the same system plotted over different markets. Of course this indicator is a ratio so it does not suffer from the usual drawback of the other absolute number ratios. Profit factor is gross profit divided by gross loss and basically reveals the size of gross profit in relation to gross loss. The higher the better. Usually a healthy trading system has a profit factor of 2, an average winning trade/average losing trade ratio of 2 and a percentage of profitable trades number equal to 50%. But there are also good systems with a profit factor of between 1.5 and 3. Think again about what you did during optmisation and your system's design and development when your profit factor goes over 3.

Drawdown

A broad definition of *drawdown* could be the largest loss or the largest losing streak of a trading system, whichever is the biggest [4]. In a more graphical way we can depict drawdown as the dip in the equity line between a highest high point and the successive lower point before a new high is made. In other words "total equity drawdown" is the open trade profits and losses plus the already closed out equity on your account. But drawdown has more subtle meanings according to whether we consider only open positions or closed out positions. In fact it is important to distinguish between three different types of drawdown:

1. An *end trade drawdown* tells us how much of the open profit we had to give back before we were allowed to exit a specific trade

2. A *close trade drawdown* is the difference between the entry and the exit price without taking into consideration what is going on within the trade

3. A *start trade drawdown* measures how much the trade went against us after the entry and before it started to go our way [6].

For sake of simplicity we will use the close trade drawdown definition since it is the most significant. But it is important to remember that while trading real money we can endure an open trade drawdown much bigger than the theoretically calculated closed trade drawdown.

It is undeniable that the absolute value of a drawdown has a deep psychological impact on the trader because he will be forced to deal with it and this could be painful. But with drawdown, as with profit indicators, we need to be careful to use this measure in a comparative way. For this purpose the concept of "underwater equity line" is useful; that is, the absolute drawdown value divided by the equity line's previous highest high value. This expresses the drawdown relative to the equity line in percentage terms. So even if we are testing a system on a 40-year long price series in which the value of the contract changed dramatically, we still have a percentage point reference value in order to spot what is the real expected drawdown at current values: just plot the highest underwater equity line percentage at the current market value.

Many analysts try to fight against drawdown by optimising the exits and the initial stops while it would be more appropriate to further understand the reason why drawdown is taking place. If there was a freak occurrence in historical terms on the markets then it is obvious that an abnormal drawdown occurred. If nothing special occurred then there is something wrong in the logic of the system.

In order to evaluate which kind of drawdown we have to worry about, and which kind of drawdown is normal, it is paramount to calculate the average drawdown and its standard deviation. If the largest drawdown lies between one and two standard deviations from the average than we should expect a future drawdown quite close to what we had in the past. If the average drawdown is beyond two standard deviations from the mean than we need to rethink the logic of the system, provided that nothing special happened in the past that could justify the freak drawdown.

The average tolerance of a drawdown for most professional traders and money managers ranges from 20% up to 30%. Let's say that a drawdown of 10% is a wonderful accomplishment while a drawdown of 30% is much more painful and worrisome. A drawdown of 40 to 50% would be unbearable for most market players.

Time averages

Other important indicators include the *time averages*. Average time in trades, according to the TradeStation terminology, displays the average time (years, days, minutes) spent in all completed trades, during the specified period for the strategy. Other trading platforms have similar indicators. Average time in trades is vital for portfolio construction since to exploit negative correlation among equity lines your systems need to be in the market at the same time or at least to have the same "average time in trades". If you make up a portfolio with a system that trades seldom and stays in the market for long periods of time, and another that trades often but with short individual trades, you will never level off the cumulative equity line.

A trading system should be balanced between the profit and risk it produces on the long side and on the short side. TradeStation split the system report between long and short trades and except in particular cases, when you can find a logical reason for it, longs should always keep pace with short in profit generation. A trading system which is not balanced in between long and short must always be regarded with suspicion.

RINA Index

A powerful indicator created by RINA Systems and included in the TradeStation trading system report is the *RINA Index*, which represents the reward-risk ratio per one unit of time and it compares the "select net profit" (net profit minus the positive and negative outlier trades, that is minus the abnormal trades that overcome the three standard deviation limit away from the average) divided by the average drawdown and again divided by the percentage of time in the market indicator (the latter is always taken from the TradeStation system report). This indicator should always be over 30 and the higher the better.

In order to measure consistency in results the TradeStation system report automatically calculates the three standard variations positive and negative limit for the average trade and for almost all the indicators. This gives an idea of how much the indicators could naturally oscillate between these boundaries. Usually the coefficient of variation (standard deviation divided by average) should never be higher than 250%.

In this paragraph we have tried to figure out some practical guidelines for a system developer without delving into much theory or philosophical considerations. Without fretting about being considered sloppy system traders we dare to openly recognise that after 20-years' experience we can understand at the first glance whether a trading system deserves to be considered with attention or not. The first aspect we check is the *equity line*, which needs to be growing smoothly and without many deep drawdowns. Personally we also appreciate many "flat times", that is parts of the equity line that are horizontal: it means that no trading was done in that period since a filter took the system out of the market. We believe that there is no need to trade continuously and a good system should know when there is some edge to be exploited over the markets and conversely when it is more appropriate to sit on the sidelines. Then, after the equity line, we immediately check average trade, profit factor, percent profitable, average win/average loss and how the monthly returns were distributed throughout the years. Just from these indicators a proper judgment about the trading system can be drawn without much worry about being on the wrong side.

2.5 Conclusion

So far we have covered the most important theoretical aspects of the trading systems' optimisation and performance evaluation. It was a quick overview of the universe of notions that this topic embraces, but we hope that this brevity will lead to a much more powerful understanding.

We can assert in conclusion that trading systems are a scientific approach to trading where nothing is left to discretion. It is not a certain business, obviously, but it is a business that deals with probability and that allows the trader to trade the markets exploiting a statistical edge.

You will be able to expand this knowledge, delving into the nuances of trading systems evaluation and optimisation, by reading the texts we included in the bibliography at the end of the book.

Unfortunately it is impossible to have a full grasp of the subject without dealing with the practical application of trading systems. Trading systems' development is not a theoretical intellectual challenge, but a practical experimental approach to markets. Writing codes, testing them and then optimising them is a process that allows the trader to acquire a practical view of the markets that is sometimes much more important than theory. Knowing how to follow this process will save much demanding work and it will help to solve situations that otherwise will be out of reach for the average trader.

In the following chapters you will have a practical view of what a systematic trader does when they develop, evaluate and optimise a trading system. We believe that this is the most important part of our work.

Part II:

Trading System Development and Evaluation of a Real Case

3

How to develop a trading system step-by-step – using the example of the British pound/US dollar pair

Introduction

The currency markets are attractive to all types of traders including individual day traders, trading companies, financial and non-financial companies, banks and governments. They trade 24 hours a day from Monday morning in New Zealand until Friday night in America. Markets with strong movements like the British pound offer you all the possibilities to develop any type of trading system from any different idea on any time scale.

In this chapter we will not present the very best trading system, which promises the highest profits. Instead our goal is to show you a trading system which is based on a sound idea and improved for a high robustness. As an aid to understanding our concept of trading system development you will find in the following pages a step-by-step explanation of how a new trading system is developed and tested for stability.

As an example we choose a trend-following system with a breakout component. We take this system and show how you can improve it up to become a profitable trading system in the following steps.

3.1 The entry logic and code. How to improve a normal moving average crossover system with a breakout filter.

3.2 Evaluation of the trading system without parameter optimisation and exits – the importance of commissions and slippage.

3.3 Variation of the input parameters: Optimisation and stability graphs.

3.4 Inserting an intraday time filter: the importance of time for short-term trading.

3.5 Determination of appropriate exits for your system by checking the development of all the system's trades. How John Sweeney's Maximum Adverse and Maximum Favourable Excursion can support you.

Let's start with the description of the logic of the system.

3.1 The birth of a trading system

As mentioned in the introduction there are lots of sources for developing your own pool of trading systems. One of them is certainly the Strategy Trading and Development Club (in short "STAD") of Omega Research (TradeStation). As a starting point we take the following entry logic, as explained in STAD, volume 13:

> The Luxor system identifies set-ups for new trades by the crossing of two moving averages
> – a fast one and a slow one. Of course, there are many types of moving averages; Luxor is
> the first strategy in STAD Club to use triangular moving averages. The purpose of the
> triangular moving average (TMA) is to increase the smoothing of the price data without
> also increasing the lag time between prices and the indicator. TMAs begin with the
> calculation of a simple arithmetic average of prices (the close is the price field most
> commonly averaged). Then, the TMA indicator calculates a simple arithmetic average of
> the first average.

So the key point in the description is the special type of moving average. When we tested the trading system we found, however, that the type of moving average did not matter and the best results were produced with a simple moving average instead of the more complex triangular moving average! So you can forget how this triangular, complex moving average works and stay with the normal ones. This confirms our observation when developing trading systems that often the simplest things work best.

The main steps in system development are the following: to get ideas which fit the personality of the traded market, to test them and to adapt them to your own needs. We do this here for the LUXOR system. We only take the main idea of how to use the moving averages and make some minor changes.

The free LUXOR system code

The programmers who want to implement this logic can find the code of the trading system in TradeStation's Easy Language below. (Other readers can skip this paragraph and continue on to the description of the trading system.) We added some comments into the code so that you know what is done and so that you can change the code easily according to your needs.

Text 3.1: Easy Language Code of the LUXOR trading system. Bold letters: Code for the entries. Normal letters: added time filter. In comment brackets: possible simple exits.

```
{Copyright 2000. OMEGA RESEARCH, INC. MIAMI, FLORIDA.
Strategy Trading and Development Club STAD, Volume 13,

Modified 18 June 2006 and 15 July 2008 by Urban Jaekle
Modified 1 January 2007 by Russell Stagg}

{1. Definition of necessary inputs and variables}

Inputs:

FastLength( 3 ),        {The input parameters of the two moving averages... }

      SlowLength( 30 ),

tset(1600),             {...start time for the intraday time window filter...}

WindowDist(100);        {...window distance for the intraday time window filter...}

                        {...can be changed – this makes optimisation possible}

Variables:              {Definition of needed variables}

      MP(0),  Fast(0),  Slow(0),  GoLong(False),  GoShort(False),  BuyStop(0),
SellStop(0), BuyLimit(0), SellLimit(0), tEnd(1700);

MP = MarketPosition;

 {2. Time window filter; see below: 3.4, "Inserting an intraday time filter"}

 tend=tset+WindowDist; {time window of 1 hour}
 if time > tset - 5 and time < tend then begin
```

{3. Definition of moving averages and entry conditions}

Fast = Average(Close, FastLength);
Slow = Average(Close, SlowLength);

GoLong = Fast > Slow;
GoShort = Fast < Slow;

{4. Entry Setup}

If Fast crosses above Slow then begin
    BuyStop = High + 1 point;
    BuyLimit = High + 5 points;
end;

If Fast crosses below Slow then begin
    SellStop = Low - 1 point;
    SellLimit= Low - 5 points;
end;

If GoLong and C < BuyLimit then
    Buy ("Long") next bar at BuyStop Stop;
If GoShort and C > SellLimit then
    Sell Short ("Short") next bar at SellStop Stop;

{5. Exits: Derived from the slow moving average. These exits are not used here since we take different standard exits! Feel free to change the exits according to your needs}

{If MP = 1 then Begin
    Sell next bar at Slow - 1 point Stop;
End;
If MP = -1 then Begin
    Buy to Cover next bar at Slow + 1 point Stop;
End;}
end;

The Easy Language Code can be divided into different parts:

1. Definition of inputs and variables

2. Time filter (discussed below in 3.4)

3. Entry and exit setup

Since this first section of this chapter focuses on the entry logic we have put the exit part of the trading system in the Easy Language Code in brackets. This means that first we leave the exits out and only take the entries from this system. Later in this chapter we use these entries and apply our own exits to them.

The entry logic

Now let's explain what this code means for the construction of the entries (Figure 3.1). The entry is based on a usual moving average system and works as following: you enter the market long on the bar where a fast moving average crosses above a slow moving average and in the same way you go short if the fast moving average crosses below the slower moving average.

Trend following methods like these are well known to be able to capture huge profits during long steady trends. The LUXOR entry logic takes this basic idea of such trend-following methods by just using two simple moving averages as an entry signal generator. However it is modified in the following way: an entry after the average crossover is only allowed after a confirmation of the price itself occurs. The crossing of the moving average alone is not enough to initiate a market position. In case of a long entry you want the current price to exceed a recent high to enter a trade (Figure 3.1). Analogously the price must go below a recent low to trigger a short entry. Please note that we only explain here the long side in the system code since the short entries are built symmetrically.

Figure 3.1: Entry Logic. The entry is not triggered by the crossing of the two moving averages. Instead, at the crossover bar the high is kept and used as a long entry level. Short entries are taken symmetrically. Chart example was taken from British pound/US dollar, 30 min, FOREX from 26 Dec 2007. Chart and datafeed from TradeStation 8.

The system has the following two input parameters which can be varied and optimised:

Inputs: FastLength (3), SlowLength (30);

These two input parameters "FastLength" and "SlowLength" are used for the fast and slow moving average:

Fast = Moving Average (Close, FastLength);
Slow = Moving Average (Close, SlowLength);

Now the important breakout filter is added. At the bar when the fast moving average crosses above the slow moving average the trade is not directly initiated. We take the high of this bar ("crossover bar", marked in red colour in Figure 3.1) and keep it as the entry stop point as long as the fast moving average stays above the slow moving average:

If Fast crosses above Slow Then EntryLevel = High;
If Fast > Slow then Buy ("Long") next bar at BuyStop Stop;

This simple but effective condition improves the probability of the simple trend following system capturing the most profitable breakouts and not just any moving average crossover which occurs. It is different to common moving average crossover systems where every trade is taken, since the additional filter has to confirm the moving averages and in this way prevents trading some false breakouts.

3.2 First evaluation of the trading system

Calculation without slippage and commissions

The strategy is now applied to 30 minute FOREX data from 21/10/2002 to 4/7/2008. All the following calculations in this chapter are based on a one contract basis. Keeping the beginning simple we calculate the trading system's results without any slippage and commissions. These will be added in the next section where we will examine their impact on system performance. Furthermore please note that at first we check the system just with entries and trade reversals, leaving out exits.

As first input parameters for the trading system's entries we choose 10 bars for the fast and 30 bars for the slow moving average. With 30 minute bars this means the fast moving average is calculated from the last 5 trading hours whereas the slow moving average relies on the last 15 hours. Figure 3.2 shows the resulting equity curve in a detailed form. With "detailed form" we mean that this curve shows all run-ups and drawdowns of the trades which happen during their lifetime. Like this the equity line is more informative compared to a form where just end-of-day or even end-of-month results are shown.

Figure 3.2: Detailed Equity Curve of the trading system LUXOR on British pound/US dollar (FOREX), 30 minute bars, 21/10/2002-4/7/2008. Input parameters: SLOW=30, FAST=10. System without exits, always in the market. Back-test without any slippage and commissions. Chart from TradeStation 8.

The equity line looks like a good starting point for a viable trading system. Although some drawdowns occur the system always recovers quickly and achieves new highs, so that you get a relatively steady growth of the initial capital. The profitability of the trading system is also revealed by the trading figures (Table 3.1). Here you see that LUXOR gains a total net profit of $66,000 with only one traded contract within the testing period from October 2002 until July 2008. The biggest drawdown within this period was $16,000. If you assume a starting capital of $30,000 then this would mean that your total profit is more than 200% in the last six years, with a maximum drawdown of about 50%.

Table 3.1: Main system figures of the LUXOR system. British pound/US dollar (FOREX), 30 minute bars, 21/10/2002-4/7/2008. Input parameters: SLOW=30, FAST=10. System without exits, always in the market. Back-test calculation without any slippage and commission.

	All Trades	Long Trades	Short Trades
Total Net Profit	$66,318	$56,918	$9,400
Gross Profit	$590,530	$310,301	$280,230
Gross Loss	($524,213)	($253,383)	($270,830)
Profit Factor	1.13	1.22	1.03
Total Number of Trades	1913	957	956
Percent Profitable	36.49%	39.81%	33.16%
Winning Trades	698	381	317
Losing Trades	1215	576	639
Avg. Trade Net Profit	$35	$59	$10
Avg. Winning Trade	$846	$814	$884
Avg. Losing Trade	($431)	($440)	($424)
Ratio Avg. Win:Avg. Loss	1.96	1.85	2.09
Largest Winning Trade	$5,628	$5,628	$4,338
Largest Losing Trade	($2,522)	($1,652)	($2,522)
Max. Consecutive Winning Trades	6	6	6
Max. Consecutive Losing Trades	16	10	11
Avg. Bars in Total Trades	37.77	39.18	36.36
Avg. Bars in Winning Trades	61.84	62.96	60.5
Avg. Bars in Losing Trades	23.94	23.45	24.38
Max. Drawdown (Intra-day Peak to Valley)	($15,644)	($11,133)	($19,746)
Date of Max. Drawdown	27-Nov-03		

The considered system shows the main properties of trend following trading strategies:

- The percentage of profitable trades is low (36.5%). From the 1913 performed trades, only 698 are profitable whereas the majority (1215) end with a loss.

- The overall gains of the system result from the high ratio of average win/average losing trade. The average winning trade is with US$846, which is bigger than the average losing trade (US$435) by a factor of two.

- The average time in winning trades is about three times longer than the average time which the system stays in losing trades (62 bars versus 24 bars).

This shows that the system logic follows perhaps the most important rule in trading which everybody knows but which is yet difficult to follow: cut the losses short and let the profits run. This trading rule is psychologically hard to adhere to since you often suffer directly from your losses and on the other hand you have to wait a long time until you can earn your rare but hefty gains.

It is worth mentioning that the long side of the trading system is much more profitable than its short side ($56,900 vs. $9,400 net profit). This observation will be examined in Chapter 5.3 again when we discuss the so called "market bias". The "market bias" means the tendency of a market to favour special features or parts of a trading system, like in this case the better profitability of the trend-following system's long side in an overall upward trend of the tested market. The good point for our trading system here is that although there is such a market bias with an up-trend, the short side of our trading system is still in the profitable range. This underlines the stability of this symmetrically built system.

Furthermore, you of course get nearly the same number of short trades (956) as long trades (957) because the trading system only reverses positions. Since we have not added any exits the system stays in the market 100% of the time, holding either a long or a short position.

Finally we want to underline a fact which should never be underestimated when developing trading systems: the statistical significance of your performed tests. If you develop a new system and in testing you have only 100 signals, or even less, the probability of achieving profitable results just by accident is very high. With nearly 2000 trades in our back-test the statistical probability is high that this strategy will perform in a similar way in the (near) future.

So what have you gained so far? Statistics show that the entry logic is sound and has a certain probability of maintaining its behaviour in the future. If you however take a closer look at the trading figures you will see that the system produces only an average profit of US$35; this level of average profit per trade without any trading costs is very low! So what you have so far is just a trading rule which detects a tiny profitable bias in prices.

Therefore we are now at a point when the trading system development work has just started. There are lots of steps to perform until you can work out a complete trading system. The profitability of this system must be increased and exits must be added. Before we do this we take trading costs into consideration to make the whole approach more realistic.

Calculation after adding slippage and commissions

When subtracting $5 of commission and $25 of slippage (which is three pips in total) per round turn from the above mentioned average per trade profit of $35 only a $5 average profit per trade is left. The detailed equity curve and the drawdown graph show the result of this more realistic calculation (Figure 3.3). Whereas the equity curve is now moving sideways with lots of oscillations, the underwater equity curve reveals big drawdowns (up to 15%) and long phases which the trading system needs to recover from these drawdowns.

Figure 3.3: Result of the trading system LUXOR with added $30 slippage and commission per round turn. A: Detailed equity curve; B: Underwater equity curve. British pound/US dollar (FOREX), 30 minute bars, 21/10/2002-4/7/2008. Input parameters: SLOW=30, FAST=10. System without exits, always in the market. Chart from TradeStation 8.

The situation for the LUXOR-trading system seems to be hopeless. With this system you are far away from gaining any profits on the pound/dollar FOREX pair. Keep in mind however that we have just chosen two arbitrary input parameters. They could be suitable or not. The key question which has to be answered now is: is this trading system useless overall, or is it a trading system that has its strengths but is suffering from the inappropriate choice of input parameters?

To answer this question more system tests like the one shown above will be necessary for multiple different input parameters. In order to prepare these tests we first want to explain what we are looking for when we perform such optimisations since there are some pitfalls to avoid.

3.3 Variation of the input parameters: optimisation and stability diagrams

What does stability of a system's input parameter mean? A short theoretical excursion

Optimisation can be your best friend but also your worst enemy when you develop a trading system. The important point is that you always know what you are doing when you vary some of the system's input parameters. Keep in mind that every trading system is in some form an optimisation. When you select a system you compare it with others and choose it because it has shown a special behaviour in the past which convinces you that this special behaviour will hold in the future. Even if you do not adjust any of its input parameters, in rejecting other, maybe similar, trading systems you have essentially done this by optimising the input parameters "afterwards" with your computer.

The open question remains: at which point does the development and selection phase of a system end and the optimisation of your system start? Since it can never be completely separated, it is better to accept that every trading system is in some way an adaptation of the past and therefore is optimised. So the key question for you as a system developer is always: which parameter do you choose from your back-tests? Which settings are likely to continue to produce profits in the future in real trading? The answer to this question is different for each trading system but one rule holds true for all: the neighbourhood of your chosen system parameters must be nearly as profitable as your chosen system parameter and the bigger this profitable parameter range is the better. Murray Ruggiero, an experienced professional trading systems developer, writes about this topic [7]:

'If you don't like the neighbouring numbers, you've got a problem, because odds are, you will wind up with the results of the neighbouring set of parameters.'

Let's have a look at an example (Figure 3.4) where we examine the hypothetical results of an imaginary system in order to select stable input parameters. On the right axis you find one input parameter of this hypothetic system which can be anything, a moving average, a distance of a stop or a profit target, a delay time etc. As a function of this system parameter you find on the vertical axis the net profit in arbitrary units.

The best input parameter of this artificial trading system in terms of net profit would be 17. With this parameter the system gained 80,000 units. But look at its neighbourhood. In the next neighbourhood, with parameter 16, the system's profit is very poor (5000 units) or with parameter 18 there is even a loss (-10,000 units). If your traded market only slightly changes in the future you will never be able to repeat this good profit which showed with parameter 17 in your back-test. So although in this hypothetical system 17 was the best parameter in the past, it is certainly not your best choice for the future.

If you, however, choose a parameter in the region between 4 and 10, e.g. 8, you are in safer territory. In that area your past net profit was not as high as your best fit parameter, but the parameters in the neighbourhood have similar profits to your chosen parameter. All gained profits are around 60,000 units. If the market changes in the future it is very likely that your trading system will still generate similar profits to those which it showed in the back-test with parameter 8 or with any other parameter between 4 and 10. So it is these broad plateaus of good (not necessarily the best!) parameters which you have to find.

Figure 3.4: Choosing stable parameters for your trading system: Net profit as a function of one system input parameter in arbitrary units. Artificially generated result of a hypothetical trading system.

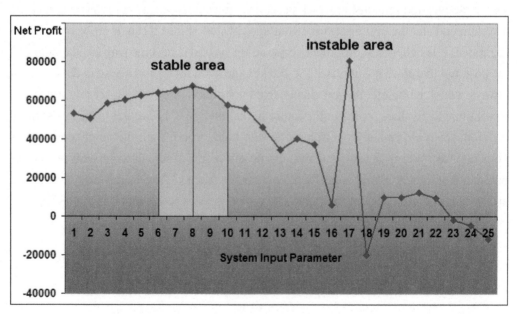

Dependency of main system figures on the two moving averages

From theory back to reality. Let's check how our trading system LUXOR behaves when changing its two input parameters, including trading costs of $30 slippage and commissions per round turn. We want to see how the results of our trend-following system change when the lengths of the fast and slow moving averages are varied. We change the two averages in a wide range, the fast moving average length from 1 bar to 20 bars in steps of 1, the slow moving average length from 21 bars to 80 bars, also in steps of 1. A fast PC computes the necessary 1200 system tests in about three minutes.

From these tests you can plot the total net profit as a function of the two varied input parameters. You can do this for each input parameter separately (as shown in Figure 3.4) but you can even do this for two system parameters in the same three-dimensional area graph (Figure 3.5). Like this you get a surface in three dimensions which show you how the input parameters affect the result of your system. With special software you can even turn this graph in every direction and look at it from different sides. Figures 3.5A and 3.5B are showing the same facts from different views. Figure 3.5A is showing the total net profit as a function of the two moving average lengths from the side, and Figure 3.5B shows the same optimisation result from above. From these two figures you see that the trading system has been profitable in a wide range of input parameter settings (dark blue areas) but has also produced losses or only small profits in other ranges of parameter settings (yellow, green and light blue areas).

Figure 3.5: Three-dimensional area diagrams for all trades of the system LUXOR. a) side view, b) top view. Net profit in US dollars as a function of the two input parameters: fast and slow moving average. Tested on British pound/US dollar (FOREX), 30 minute bars, 21/10/2002-4/7/2008, incl. $30 S+C per RT. Diagrams generated with RINA 3D Smart View.

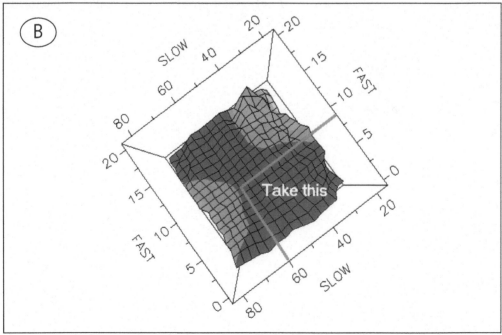

Of course we are looking for input parameters which produced a high net profit in the past. But as shown above in Figure 3.4 it is even more important for those system parameters that they have enough peer parameters in their near neighbourhood which were nearly as profitable as the chosen "best" ones. In our trading system which we have developed, so far the whole area in the lower right part (Figure 3.5B) seems at a first glance to fulfil this requirement. We'll now take this shorter area and have a closer look on it (Figures 3.6A-D). From these graphs you can see that the system stays very stable against parameter variation in the chosen area. Although the total net profit varies in a relatively big range (between $20,000 and $100,000) it stays clearly positive for all selected input parameters. The best profits of nearly $100,000 are achieved in the region when the fast moving average is very small (< 3) and the slow moving average is between 30-50. This is also the area with the smallest maximum intraday drawdowns of about $15,000. Over all parameters the maximum intraday drawdown does vary quite a lot but never becomes excessive – it always stays below about $35,000.

Like the total net profit and the maximum intraday drawdown you can plot further important statistical figures as a function of the two input parameters (Figures 3.6C and D). If you do so you get further valuable insight into your trading system. If you watch, for example, the total number of trades of the system (Figure 3.6D) you can see a fact which holds true for many trend following systems: the slower you make them to react (in our case the longer the look-back periods of the two moving averages are) the less trades you get. By changing the input parameters of the system you have the possibility of affecting some key attributes which allows you to adapt a system better to your trading style or to the requirements of a money management scheme in a bigger portfolio. Let's say you have many fast-reacting systems in your portfolio and need more slow-reacting components – you may achieve this by choosing longer look-back periods for the moving averages. If you need a faster-reacting system you make the input parameters smaller. We'll come back to this observation in our portfolio building section when correlations between different trading systems and their different time scales become important.

Interestingly, in our trading system, while the number of trades changes a lot with the system's input parameters, another trading figure, the average profit per trade, stays relatively stable (Figure 3.6C). It varies between $10 and $50 but mostly stays between $30 and $40, especially for all fast moving averages between 1 and 9 and the slower averages between 30 and 50.

From these results you can conclude that "good" system parameters will be an instantaneously reacting fast moving average (< 3) and a slow moving average between

30 and 50. Let's take the value "1" as input value for the fast moving average. It is clear that a one period moving average is not a real moving average, even if for the sake of simplicity we keep calling it a moving average. In fact the fast moving average becomes the closing price itself. For the slower average you can take any value between 30 and 50. We choose here 44 as an input value since it produces the highest total net profit and has a wide neighbourhood of profitable parameters.

Of course you should always observe the behaviour of your system in the following months and if it turns out after a longer period of screening that the chosen parameters (1/44) are not the most stable choice then you must change them, for example to 3/30 (if these parameters proved to be more stable than your initial choice of 1/44). Such a parameter change is an example of a reoptimisation. You will find a more systematic approach to the topic of periodic reoptimisation and walk forward optimisation in Chapter 6. For the moment we stay with the parameters of 1 (fast moving average) and 44 (slow moving average) and we will take a closer look at the trading system's performance.

Figure 3.6: Three-dimensional area diagrams for all trades of the trading system LUXOR. Main system figures as a function of the two input parameters: fast and slow moving average. Tested on British pound/US dollar (FOREX), 30 minute bars, 21/10/2002-4/7/2008, including $30 S+C per RT. A: net profit B: maximum intraday drawdown C: average trade net profit D: number of total trades generated. Diagrams generated with RINA 3D Smart View.

(B)

(C)

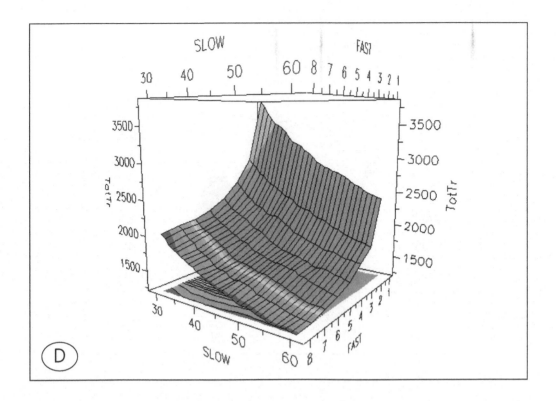

Result with optimised input values

With the fast moving average set to 1 bar (=closing price itself) and the slow moving average set to 44 bars you get a steadily growing equity curve (Figure 3.7A). This result is confirmed with the underwater-equity curve which always quickly recovers after every drawdown (Figure 3.7B). The biggest drawdown happened in November 2003. It was, with 8%, only half as big as the drawdown of more than 15% which we got with the non-optimised input parameters (10/30).

Figure 3.7: Trading system LUXOR, tested on British pound/US dollar (FOREX), 30 minute bars, 21/10/2002-4/7/2008. Optimised input parameters in terms of net profit: SLOW=44, FAST=1. System without exits, always in the market, long or short. Back-test includes $30 slippage and commission. Chart from TradeStation 8. A: Detailed equity curve; B: Weekly underwater equity curve.

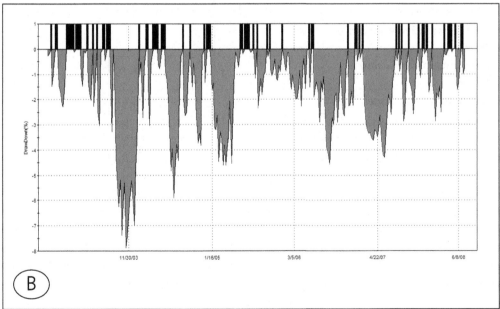

Table 3.2: Main system figures of the trading system LUXOR. British pound/US dollar (FOREX), 30 minute bars, 21/10/2002-4/7/2008. Input parameters: SLOW=44, FAST=1. System without exits, always in the market. Back-test includes $30 slippage and commission per round turn.

	All Trades	Long Trades	Short Trades
Total Net Profit	$100,125	$73,888	$26,237
Gross Profit	$666,862	$347,323	$319,540
Gross Loss	($566,738)	($273,435)	($293,303)
Profit Factor	1.18	1.27	1.09
Total Number of Trades	2980	1490	1490
Percent Profitable	26.41%	28.26%	24.56%
Winning Trades	787	421	366
Losing Trades	2193	1069	1124
Avg. Trade Net Profit	$33.60	$49.59	$17.61
Avg. Winning Trade	$847	$825	$873
Avg. Losing Trade	($258)	($256)	($261)
Ratio Avg. Win:Avg. Loss	3.28	3.23	3.35
Largest Winning Trade	$5,428	$5,428	$4,418
Largest Losing Trade	($2,062)	($2,062)	($1,452)
Max. Consecutive Winning Trades	7	7	7
Max. Consecutive Losing Trades	24	18	21
Avg. Bars in Total Trades	24.69	25.61	23.77
Avg. Bars in Winning Trades	60.75	60.82	60.66
Avg. Bars in Losing Trades	11.75	11.75	11.76
Max. Drawdown (Intra-day Peak to Valley)	($13,440)	($7,594)	($19,284)
Date of Max. Drawdown	26-Nov-03		

Although the overall return/drawdown ratio of the LUXOR system is acceptable a closer look at the system figures reveals that the system we have developed to this point cannot be traded yet (Table 3.2). Although the system obviously shows a bias in the prices and the trading system is robust the average trade, with $33, is still not very profitable.

Furthermore, the system stays in the market 100% of the time because the exits are still missing. As a consequence the system is not useable in this state since the risks would be too high compared with the prospective returns. Therefore in the next two chapters we will further extend our trading system.

First we will look for useful intraday time filters in order to increase the system's profitability. The final section of this chapter will deal with adding the necessary exits.

3.4 Inserting an intraday time filter

In the past we have come across many master traders and profitable trading systems which exploit the different behaviours of financial markets during different phases within the trading day. There are traders and systems which are just successful in the afternoon with short-term breakout strategies and there are others which need their slow trend-following strategies running the whole night in order to make profits. The reason for the importance of the factor "time" in your trading strategies is simply that markets are controlled by people and people are constricted by their daily time schedule. Since the currency markets are trading 24 hours, the time of the day has a special importance for their behaviour. There will be differences if the big US traders are active or not, if it is night or day in Europe, in the US or in Asia. The daily FOREX volume clearly shows that the market activity changes a lot within each trading day. There are market phases of more activity and higher probability for profits and there are quiet market phases when nothing happens except accidental sideways movements with high market noise. As a consequence it is always worth examining how different time filters change the outcome of your trading system, especially when dealing with currency markets like the pound and dollar[3].

Finding the best entry time

We now perform system tests in the following way. We take our LUXOR entry but we restrict the entry times to a short 4-hour time window every day. We will shift the starting time of the window in steps of 30 minutes throughout the day in order to find the best window. (For the Easy Language Programmers: you have to add some lines into the LUXOR-code as shown above, Text 3.1, point 2, Time Window Filter.)

---

[3] Time investigations are valuable for many other markets. Some of you might have read our article in *Traders* magazine [8] where we presented two short-term trading systems based on 5 minute and 20 minute intraday data for the European and US Stock Index Futures.

Figure 3.8 shows the total net profit of the trading system as a function of the starting time of the 4-hour time window. And the result is really significant! You see that the profit of our trading system highly depends on the chosen time window. When you start trading from 5pm until 3am Greenwich Mean Time (GMT) the trading system loses money, whereas it is able to gain high profits during GMT day time, especially in the morning between 8am and 12am.

Figure 3.8: Total Net Profit as a function of the entry time of a 4-hour time window. LUXOR system, tested on British pound/US dollar (FOREX), 30 minute bars, 21/10/2002-4/7/2008. SLOW=44, FAST=1. Calculation incl. $30 S+C per RT. No exits are in place.

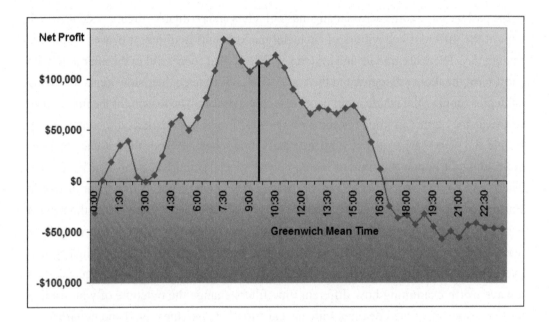

The highest net profit is earned when you take 7.30am as the starting point for your time window, and this means that you only allow entries and reversals from 7:30am until 11.30am. From our above discussion about stability and robustness of input parameters you know, however, that it is important that your chosen system parameter has a good and broad neighborhood. With this neighbourhood the trading system has the highest reliability of conforming to its back-test results in real trading. Therefore we take the starting time of the window right in the middle of the profitable parameter region at 9.30am, instead of the most profitable value at 7.30am. The chosen time filter means that we allow entries only between 9.30am and 1.30pm GMT. This is the time when the big volume from the US in the afternoon (GMT time) is still to come. It seems to be good for our trading system to enter a trend in the beginning of the day which later can be amplified by increasing volume from the US.

Result with added time filter

The detailed equity curve of our trading system seems not to have changed a lot because of the added time filter (Figure 3.9A). Instead, a look at the underwater equity curve reveals that the drawdowns within the 5 years of trading have increased from 8% before to 10% with the daytime filter. Furthermore, it now takes longer for our modified trading system to recover from these drawdowns. So what have we gained from our filter? You can evaluate the time filter impact with a closer look at the trading figures. If you look at the number of trades you see that they have been reduced dramatically by the inserted filter to 902, compared with nearly 3000 trades which the system generated before. Together with the fact that the total net profit slightly increased to $115,000, compared with $100,000 without the time filter, this leads to a very important point for you when using this system:

The average profit per trade is now $128 (including $30 slippage and commissions) compared with the poor $33 which the system had gained before when trading was allowed around the clock. This is an improvement by a factor of four!

Figure 3.9: LUXOR system results with added time filter. Entries only allowed in the 4-hour time window from 9.30am–1.30pm GMT. A: detailed equity curve. B: weekly underwater equity curve. British pound/US dollar (FOREX), 30 minute bars, 21/10/2002-4/7/2008. Optimised input parameters in terms of net profit: SLOW=44, FAST=1. Test without exits. Back-test includes $30 slippage and commission. Charts from TradeStation 8.

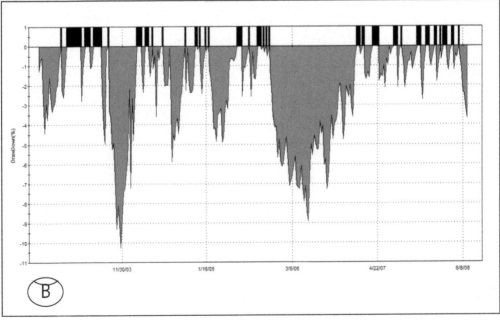

Table 3.3: Main system figures of the LUXOR system with added time filter: Entries only allowed in the 4-hour time window from 9.30am– 1.30pm GMT. British pound/US dollar (FOREX), 30 minute bars, 21/10/2002-4/7/2008. Optimised input parameters: SLOW=44, FAST=1. System without exits, always in the market, long or short. Back-test includes $30 slippage and commission.

	All Trades	Long Trades	Short Trades
Total Net Profit	$115,502	$82,050	$33,452
Gross Profit	$428,864	$226,323	$202,541
Gross Loss	($313,362)	($144,273)	($169,089)
Profit Factor	1.37	1.57	1.2
Total Number of Trades	902	451	451
Percent Profitable	42.02%	44.79%	39.25%
Winning Trades	379	202	177
Losing Trades	523	249	274
Avg. Trade Net Profit	$128	$182	$74
Avg. Winning Trade	$1,132	$1,120	$1,144
Avg. Losing Trade	($599)	($579)	($617)
Ratio Avg. Win:Avg. Loss	1.89	1.93	1.85
Largest Winning Trade	$6,748	$6,748	$5,728
Largest Losing Trade	($2,531)	($2,531)	($2,442)
Max. Consecutive Winning Trades	6	7	6
Max. Consecutive Losing Trades	13	8	11
Avg. Bars in Total Trades	78.82	78.44	79.2
Avg. Bars in Winning Trades	116.73	113.29	120.66
Avg. Bars in Losing Trades	51.34	50.16	52.41
Total Slippage	$18,040	$9,020	$9,020
Total Commission	$9,020	$4.510	$4.510
Percent of Time in the Market	99.92%		
Max. Drawdown (Intra-day Peak to Valley)	$18,894	$9,402	$17,378
Date of Max. Drawdown	24-May-06		

But in spite of these promising trade figures the system still has some major weak points.

As we already mentioned the drawdowns have become slightly bigger – $18,900 maximum drawdown compared with $13,400 before. But this drawback and the fact that the trading system equity is not as steady as before are not the worst features. The weak point of the trading system in its current state is simply that it is really dangerous since trade reversals are only allowed in the four-hour window between 9.30am and 1.30pm GMT. If you get a reversal signal outside of this window, e.g. in the night at 1am GMT, since the market is closed the system cannot exit or reverse its position. Outside of your trading window you have to stay in the market for the other 20 hours, regardless of what happens. Of course the system is not tradeable like this since the limitations and the risks of the system would be too high if you are forced to stay in the market for 20 hours irrespective of any developments during that time. We have to urgently change this situation and extend our trading system by adding exits. By adding exits we want to create not only a profitable trading system, but also one which can be controlled in terms of risk.

3.5 Determination of appropriate exits – risk management

Look at it this way: whether your trading system resembles a gunslinger shooting from the hip or a well-aimed sniper lying in ambush, knowing where your trades are heading could mean the difference between riding into the sunset or lying fatally wounded on a dusty street at high-noon. To stay alive you must know when to draw and when to run.

Thomas Stridsman [1]

Everybody knows that stops are necessary but nobody really likes them. Often you get the feeling that the stop has just thrown you out of the market before it turned in your direction and you missed the big move.

In this section we use statistical research to investigate exits quantitatively. In the course of all of our past statistical investigations it has become obvious that an exit can never be considered independently from the relative entry. It's important to be aware that the dynamics of the entry have a substantial influence on the dynamics of a useful exit or a reversal of your position. Imagine an entry into a quiet, not volatile market with low trading volume and compare it with an entry which was triggered during a phase of high activity, e.g. a "news-breakout" (Figure 3.10). In the first case it could be best to take profits at a close profit target as the market moves sideways without any direction. In the second case a wide stop and no profit target could be much better since these two exits give the trade enough room to develop. Every profit target or stop which is placed too close would throw you out of the profitable trade too early. The "best" exit in this case would be the end-of-day exit when the big trading volume has diminished and the breakout has obviously finished.

For this reason we don't recommend testing exits with artificially generated entries, e.g. with random entries or with entries taken at the opening of every trading day. We found that working with such random entries leads the statistical results into a wrong direction. The outcome is dominated by market situations which occur most of the time but which are not the typical ones applicable to your own, special market strategy.

Figure 3.10: The Dynamic of Exits. In the phase of low volume and low volatility different exits are needed than in the phase of increasing volume with the short breakout. Chart example was taken from Light Crude Oil, 5 minute, NYMEX from 22 August 2008. Chart and datafeed from TradeStation 8.

There are no universal optimal exits! If you are working with a different type of system or on another time scale you cannot transfer your existing exits to a different entry logic. Of course you can take such exits as a rough guide but you must spend time developing suitable exits for the different entry or time scale.

To find appropriate exits for the strategy developed above we take a small excursion into the field of statistics. We analyse the course of the single trades in order to determine useful stop-levels and profit targets. This analysis looks a little bit exotic at the beginning. As soon as you are familiar with it, however, you'll be rewarded with a good understanding of your trading system and its appropriate exits.

The concept of Maximum Adverse Excursion (MAE)

In order to find proper stop points for your system you should take a deeper look into the distribution of trades and examine each trade individually. When you do so, you will discover that there are similarities between them, but that every trade also has its own set of characteristics. These characteristics can be examined by using the Maximum Adverse Excursion (MAE) technique developed by John Sweeney less than ten years ago [9]. MAE is defined as the most intraday price movement against your position. In other words it's the lowest open equity during the lifespan of a trade. The MAE concept allows you to evaluate your systems' individual trades to determine at what dollar or percentage amount to place your protective stop.

Let's take a look at the MAE graphic of our trading system (Figure 3.11). This graph shows all 902 trades that are produced within the tested period. For each trade you can see the amount of drawdown that occurred in relation to the realised profit or loss. The winning trades are shown as green up arrows and the losing trades are represented as red down arrows. On the vertical y-axis of the MAE diagram you see the final profit whereas the horizontal x-axis shows the intraday drawdown of each trade.

Since we are using this graphic to determine where to place our stops we have put all the winning and losing trades on the same cluster graph. This means that although trades A and B in Figure 3.11 appear to be similar they are in reality quite different. Trade A had a drawdown of $2400 and closed at a final loss of $1000. Trade B, on the other hand, suffered an even bigger drawdown of $2500 but recovered and managed to end with a gain of $1000. Whether the dollar amount indicated along the y-axis is a profit or loss is determined by the colour and the direction of the small triangles. Keeping the trades clustered on the same graph makes it easier to figure out how much unrealised loss must be incurred by a trade before it typically does not recover. In this way the MAE graphic tells you when to cut your loss because the risks associated with the trade are no longer justified. This gives you a valuable indication of where to place your protective stop.

Figure 3.11: The MAE graph of LUXOR system. Green: winning trades, red: losing trades. System tested on British pound/US dollar (FOREX), 30 minute bars, 21/10/2002-4/7/2008, with entry time window 9.30am-1.30pm GMT. Input parameters SLOW=44, FAST=1. Without exits, always in the market, including $30 S+C per RT. Diagram created with TradeStation 8.

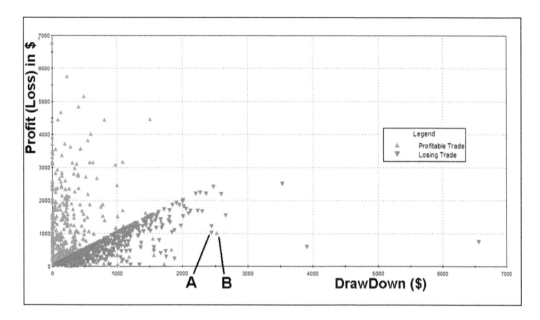

In order to decide where to put this stop we show the same MAE graph in percentage terms (Figure 3.12A). We switch to percentage terms since the percentage display gives a better adaptation to changing market conditions than fixed dollar values. Especially on markets with big point value changes the advantages of the percentage based calculation become obvious. In such conditions it is better to work with exits that are adapting to the current market value instead of staying fixed and inflexible.

Figure 3.12A: MAE graph in percentage terms. Green up arrows = winning trades, red down arrows = losing trades. Trend-following system British pound/US dollar (FOREX), 30 minute bars, 21/10/2002-4/7/2008, with entry time window 9.30am-1.30pm GMT. Input parameters SLOW=44, FAST=1. Without exits, always in the market, including $30 S+C per RT. Diagram created with TradeStation 8.

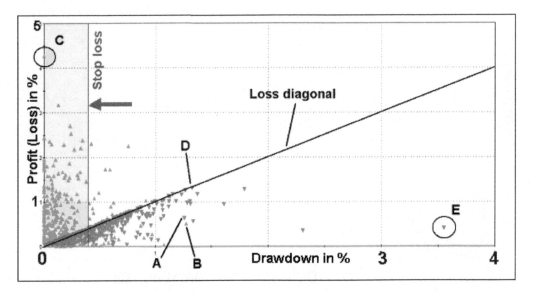

Figure 3.12B: Maximum Adverse Excursion graph in percentage terms after inserting a 0.3% stop loss into the system. LUXOR system tested on British pound/US dollar (FOREX), 30 minute bars, 21/10/2002-4/7/2008, with entry time window 9.30am-1.30pm GMT. Input parameters SLOW=44, FAST=1. Diagram created with TradeStation 8.

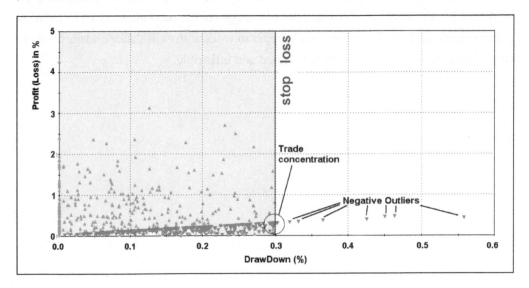

Let us briefly explain some trades from the MAE diagram in order to become more familiar with it. First you see that the relative positions of trade A and B explained above have changed. Trade A is now on a higher position in y-direction since the two trades took place in different times when the market was trading at a different level. Because the calculation is now based on percentage of the underlying market, the same dollar values usually mean different percentage values.

When watching all these 902 trades in the MAE diagram you can see some characteristics of the trading system. The first point is that on the left side of the diagram you find more winning than losing trades. This is clear since winning trades usually don't suffer such big drawdowns as losing trades. The "best" trades for you are obviously the ones which behave like trade C – trades that are profitable from the beginning without suffering any negative open equity in their lifetime and are placed on the very left side close to the y-axis of the diagram (profit/loss axis).

Another interesting area of trades is what we call the "loss diagonal". On this characteristic line you can find a lot of losing trades. Like trade D all these trades ended with a loss which represents their biggest drawdowns. On the other hand, trades like E also exist. This trade suffered a big drawdown of over 3.5% from the entry-point but recovered from this position to a final loss of only about 0.5%.

Now we want to place a protective stop loss at a certain distance (percentage of market value) away from the entry point in order to limit the risk of the trade. How does the MAE diagram help you to determine a good distance for this added stop?

Let us look how the MAE diagram helps to understand what an inserted stop loss does in your trading system.

The stop loss in the MAE diagram can be drawn as a vertical line. Such a stop loss theoretically cuts all trades that suffer a bigger loss from their entry than this set stop loss (Figure 3.12B). In the MAE diagram this means that the stop loss prohibits all the trades on the right of the 0.3% line and moves them to this line. This sounds good for all the losses (red points) that are made smaller by this stop. But think about all the winning trades. They are turned into a red spot, a loss of 0.3%, as soon as they reach the stop loss and never get the chance to become a winning trade.

We try to place a stop in an area that captures the majority of winning trades while simultaneously limiting the strategy's exposure to profit erosion. Obviously it is good to set a stop loss so as to cut as many trades which end on the loss diagonal as possible without affecting trades that end as winners, or at least those trades that recover from their lowest points.

So the question is what happens if you make the stop loss smaller than 0.6%, going to 0.4%, 0.3% or even 0.1%? Obviously you will then cut more and more trades that are ending on the loss diagonal and for which the stop loss does a good job in cutting them early enough. But the more you move your stop loss to the left side, the more trades you also cut which recovered from their biggest drawdowns or which even ended as winning trades.

Inserting a risk stop loss

In the MAE diagram you can see how all trades behaved and if there are any special points to consider when looking for a good place to set a proper risk stop loss. The MAE diagram can give you a hint that the "optimal" stop value is somewhere between 0.2% and 1%. However MAE does not tell you directly what the optimal value is to set this stop. For this reason we now look at the task from a different side by performing system tests in the following way. We add a risk stop loss into our trading system and vary its distance in reference to the trade's entry point in a wide range from 0.01% up to 1% in steps of 0.01%. At the time of writing the British pound was trading near US$2.00 and at this rate a 1% stop distance corresponds to 2 cents. Two cents are in other words 200 pips and mean $2000 in your pocket. Therefore the fine 0.01% step means 0.02 cents or 2 pips ($20 in your pocket) in these market conditions.

Figure 3.13: Ratio of total net profit/maximum intraday drawdown as a function of the stop loss distance in per cent. LUXOR system tested on British pound/US dollar (FOREX), 30 minute bars, 21/10/2002-4/7/2008, with entry time window 9.30am-1.30pm GMT. SLOW=44, FAST=1. Including $30 S+C per RT.

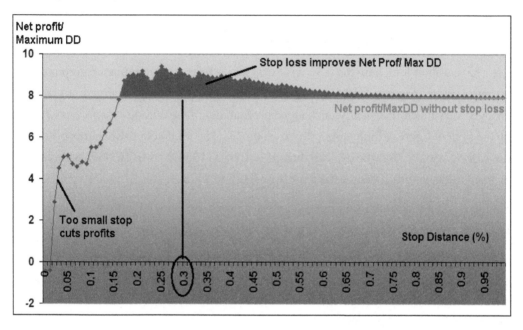

The tests give you important statistical figures for each stop level: net profit, maximum drawdown, biggest losing trade etc. You can draw diagrams of these figures dependent on the set stop loss distance. We do this here for the ratio of total net profit/maximum drawdown (NP/DD), see Figure 3.13. We do not take the total net profit alone because it does not tell you much about the system's risk, whereas the ratio NP/DD gives a meaningful estimate. Let's look at this ratio for all performed trades as a function of the stop distance. This graph tells you that stop loss points positioned too closely reduce the NP/DD ratio drastically. Obviously many trades are stopped out just at the beginning and the slippage and commissions do not allow gains with so little risk.

When increasing the distance more and more the system becomes profitable, but for all stop distances below 0.15% the NP/DD ratio is still decreased and stays below the ratio of the breakout-system without stop loss. However, if you set the stop futher away from the entry point and allow the trades more room to develop you get a nice improvement of the NP/DD. Any added stop in a broad range of values between 0.2-0.5% range increases the base system's return/risk ratio. Thus we can select a stop loss of 0.3% as a useful distance – this value is placed in the middle of this stable parameters region. The 0.3% corresponds to 60 pips or 600 US dollars with the British pound trading at US$2. It is important to mention that you cannot find a stop loss level that improves the overall net profit for every trading system or market. Usually profits are reduced by the boundaries which are imposed by the stop losses, especially in more choppy markets (e.g. in stock index futures like S&P 500 or FTSE 100).

Let's have a short look how the 0.3% risk stop loss affects the performance graphs of our trading system (Figures 3.14A and B). The detailed equity curve seemed not to have changed very much. The nearly unchanged profitability of the trading system is confirmed by the system figures (Table 3.4, left two columns). The total net profit is improved with the stop loss only slightly by less than 1% from $115,000 to $116,000, whereas the average trade net profit decreased a bit from $128 to $113.

So, the profitability of the trading system stays nearly unchanged with the inserted stop loss. But let's check if the risks of the system are now under better control.

Figure 3.14A: Detailed equity curve, B: underwater equity curve with 0.3% risk stop loss in place. LUXOR system tested on British pound/US dollar (FOREX), 30 minute bars, 21/10/2002-4/7/2008, with entry time window 9.30am-1.30pm GMT. SLOW=44, FAST=1. Including 30 $ S+C per RT. Charts from TradeStation 8.

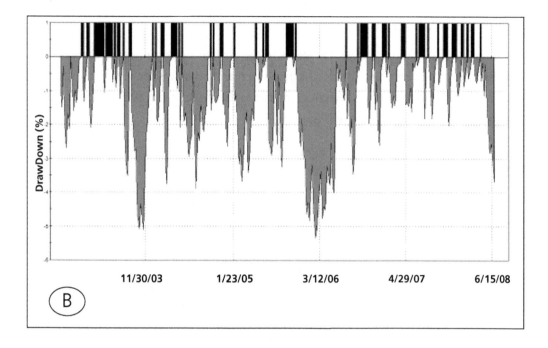

From the underwater equity curves you see that the maximum drawdown of the trading system is now reduced from 10% to 5% (compare Figure 3.14B with 3.9B). A look at the trading figures confirms this observation (Table 3.4, page 82).

After inserting the risk stop loss the maximum intraday peak-to-valley drawdown is much reduced from $18,894 to $11,266. Even more importantly, the largest losing trade is now reduced to only $810 from over $2500 when using the system without the stop loss in place. This significant reduction by nearly a factor of three helps you to control your risks, especially when trading the system with more than one lot in a bigger portfolio. You may ask why the biggest loss was not reduced to about $600, which corresponds to the 0.3% in today's market value, set by our stop loss. The reason was a gap which inhibited an execution of a trade at the exact stop price but at a US$250 worse price. Although such bad executions usually happen less than 10 times within 1000 trades, which is insignificant and well covered with the $30 slippage and commissions calculation, you have to keep in mind that this is always possible in general with every trade. Finally, we want to point out that the system's market exposure with the inserted stop was reduced for the first time. Whereas without any exit in place the system was in the market 100% of the time, this risk exposure is now reduced to 73%. The remaining 27% of the time while the system is not active can be used to invest the money somewhere else or to earn interest gains.

Adding a trailing stop

A trailing stop is a stop order which adapts to the current market price. In the case of a new long position it is initially set at a fixed percentage below the entry price. If the market price rises, the trailing stop price rises proportionately, but if the price falls, the trailing stop price doesn't change (Figure 3.15A).

Figure 3.15A: The principle of a trailing stop. Chart example from British pound/US dollar (FOREX), 30 minute bars, September 2008. Chart from TradeStation 8.

The trailing stop for short positions works analogously. This technique allows you to set a limit on the maximum possible loss without setting a limit on the maximum possible gain. Next we add such a trailing stop to our existing trading system. While looking for an appropriate trailing stop distance, we keep our initial risk stop loss of 0.3% in place. Whereas this initial risk stop is responsible for keeping the biggest losses under control, as outlined in the previous section, the now added trailing stop aims at keeping some more profit without losing it again.

If you add such a trailing stop and vary its distance from 0.01% up to 1.5% in steps of 0.01% you can plot the ratio of NP/DD as a function of the trailing stop distance (Figure 3.15B). Similar to the risk stop loss, tiny trailing stops cut the profits too much, since they don't give the trades enough room to develop. In particular, all trailing stop values below 0.2% lead to a disaster. However from 0.2 to 0.5% the results increase steadily and between 0.5% and 1% you find a broad region of trailing stops which increase the system's NP/DD ratio. If you set the trailing stops even wider then the ratio converges to the NP/DD ratio of the trading system without an added trailing stop. The stop distance becomes so big that fewer and fewer trades are affected by it.

Figure 3.15B: Ratio of total net profit/maximum intraday drawdown as a function of the distance of an added trailing stop. Risk stop loss of 0.3% kept in place. LUXOR system tested on British pound/US dollar (FOREX), 30 minute bars, 21/10/2002-4/7/2008, with entry time window 9.30am-1.30pm GMT. SLOW=44, FAST=1. Including $30 S+C per RT.

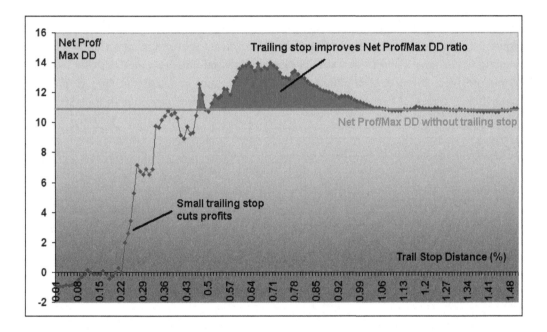

It is worth mentioning that the NP/DD ratio (Figure 3.15B) is quite steady. Between 0.5% and 1% you find a broad region of values which lead to similar results. This increases the probability that the performed tests have a high predictive power for real trading. The trading figures (Table 3.4, on page 82, third column) reveal that a trailing stop of 0.8% (in the middle of the profitable area) leads to improvements, especially regarding profitability. The total net profit can be increased by the inserted trailing stop from $116,209 to $126,772 by nearly 10%. The average profit per trade increases by about the same percentage from $113 to $122. The risk figures are also slightly improved by the added trailing stop. The maximum drawdown of the trading system is further reduced from $11,266 to $10,292 and the percentage of time in the market is also now slightly lower (69.98%, compared to 73.56% before).

With the two types of stops in place we will now check if inserting profit targets will further improve the trading system.

Looking for profit targets: Maximum Favourable Excursion (MFE)

John Sweeney's concept of MFE is complementary to MAE. MFE is defined as the most positive price movement for your position. It therefore corresponds to the highest open equity within the lifespan of a trade. Whereas MAE was useful to investigate your trades' drawdowns and to set a good stop loss, MFE reveals their run-ups and helps to find useful profit targets (Figure 3.16).

Figure 3.16: The MFE graph shows the realised profit/loss vs. run-ups of all trades. Green: winning trades, red: losing trades. LUXOR system tested on British pound/US dollar (FOREX), 30 minute bars, 21/10/2002-4/7/2008, with 0.3% risk stop and 0.8% trailing stop. Input parameters SLOW=44, FAST=1, including $30 S+C per RT. Diagram created with TradeStation 8.

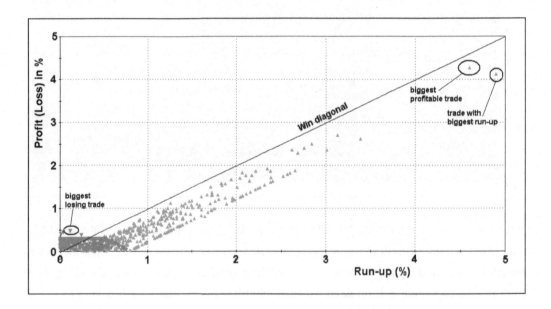

Like with MAE, the final profit (or loss) of the trades is shown on the vertical y-axis. Again winning and losing trades are drawn on this same axis with different colour (green points=winning trades, red points=losing trades). But in contrast to the MAE diagram, in the MFE diagram the horizontal x-axis represents the run-up, which means the highest profit a trade has had in its lifetime.

From the MFE diagram of the original trend-following system with the two exits in place (stop loss=0.3%, trailing stop=0.8%) you can spot the following features:

Most winning trades end near the win diagonal, which marks the points where a trade ended with the highest intraday run-up. The biggest profitable trade is a typical example. It had an intraday run-up of 4.5% and ended near this highest value with a final profit of just above 4%. Further, the MFE diagram shows the effect of the 0.8% trailing stop which we inserted in the last section: all trades that experienced a profit of more than 0.8% were kept profitable – the trailing stop makes sure that the highly profitable trades cannot completely reverse their direction. The MFE diagram also reveals that the losing trades (red points) stay mostly on the very left side. This means that they usually had only small run-ups.

These findings suggest that profit targets cannot be very effective for our trend following system with the two stops already at work. If a losing trade never comes into a big profit and if winning trades don't significantly change their direction then a profit target will not be helpful. Inserted profit targets cannot find a point to skim profits out of the market before it turns.

Let's verify if these findings can stand further computer tests. We take our basic breakout system with the two stops and add a profit target. The target closes each trade immediately if a profit of x percent of the market value is reached (Figure 3.17). The figure shows that profit targets placed too closely, like stops that are too small, reduce the overall profits of the trading system. The closer you set the profit target the worse it gets. Only a small region of quite big profit targets around 2% (=4 cents or 400 pips conditions or $4000 for one contract, with the pound trading at $2) lead to a profit bigger than our system with just the stops and no target in place. If you place the targets even higher than 2.5% away from the entry point you finally reach the result of the base system. The MFE diagram shows that this area of very high profits can only be reached by less than 10% trades. Therefore profit targets to exit a trade are only of small use for our entry set-up on the British pound/US dollar FOREX market.

Figure 3.17: Ratio of total net profit/maximum intraday drawdown as a function of the distance of an added profit target. Risk stop loss of 0.3% and trailing stop of 0.8% are kept in place during tests. LUXOR system tested on British pound/US dollar (FOREX), 30 minute bars, 21/10/2002-4/7/2008, with entry time window 9.30am-1.30pm GMT. SLOW=44, FAST=1. Including. $30 S+C per RT.

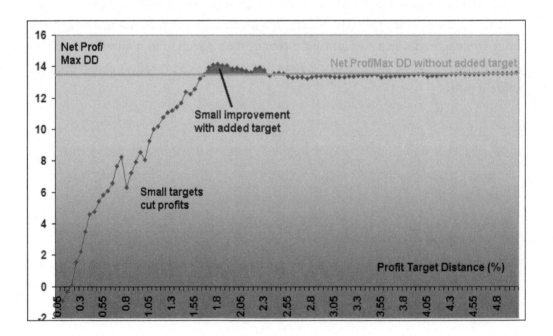

The tests confirmed what the MFE diagram showed: it is not possible to predict how far the breakout will lead the market. Therefore, except with targets between about 1.8% and 2.4% away from the entry point, it is better not to set any profit targets but just let the market run as far it goes. Again, like with the stop loss, this conclusion may not hold true for other markets with the same trading system or for the British pound/US dollar FOREX on other time scales with completely different entry set-up. One example where profit targets are more rewarding is stock index futures, where changes in trend direction happen more often. Furthermore, profit targets become more valuable if they are set to significant points, e.g. at supports and resistances, gaps etc, where the market is more likely to turn. Another reason why profit targets are useful will be discussed at the end of this chapter in a short section on money management.

Summary: Result of the entry logic with the three added exits

You can determine your stop and profit target levels in your trading system alone with classical optimisation tests, as shown in Figures 3.13, 3.15B, and 3.17. Such optimisations show you optimal stop and target levels and give you valuable information about the stability of the optimal parameters we found. However, such diagrams do not show you how the final net profit and drawdown have emerged. You cannot see from such graphs if one single highly profitable trade or a hundred small winners are responsible for the total net profit of your trading system. This missing valuable information about the distribution of all your trades is only provided by the MAE/MFE diagrams. They show you in one single chart all the trades' intraday run-ups and drawdowns. In this way the MAE/MFE method provides useful additional information about your trading system and complements the optimisation graphs.

Therefore, in this chapter we used a combination of optimisation graphs and MAE/MFE diagrams in order to determine useful stop levels and profit targets for the LUXOR system. For the British pound/US dollar FOREX market our tests showed that stop losses and trailing stops placed widely enough did a good job in reducing the risks of the system while also slightly increasing its profits. The profit target which we added finally is not necessary and helps just a little bit, if placed in the area around 2%. Let's have a look at the results of our trading system with all the above developed and discussed exits in place: 0.3% risk stop, 0.8 trailing stop and 1.9% profit target (Figures 3.18A-C).

Figure 3.18: LUXOR system with all three exits in place: 0.3% risk stop, 0.8% trailing stop and 1.9% profit target, tested on British pound/US dollar (FOREX), 30 minute bars, 21/10/2002-4/7/2008, with entry time window 9.30am-1.30pm GMT. SLOW=44, FAST=1. Including $30 S+C per RT. A: detailed equity curve, B: end of month equity curve, C: average profit per month. Charts created with TradeStation 8.

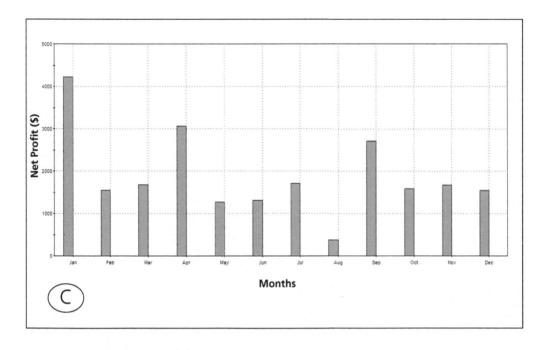

Months

C

The detailed equity curve seems not to have changed a lot if you compare it with the equity curve without added exits (Figure 3.19A). It just looks a bit steadier with fewer and less sharp drawdowns. The biggest drawdown is now 6% (compared with 10% with no exits in place) and the system always quickly recovers to new equity highs within some weeks. The longest recovery period from any drawdown was 6 months. This is also confirmed with the end of month equity curve which plots the account value of the traded money once per month. If you sort the profits by different months from January until December you can see that the trading system was profitable in all months (Figure 3.18C), which is another proof for its reliability. These findings are also underlined with the trading system's figures calculated with all the exits in place (Table 3.4, right column). One remarkable point is that the 1.9% profit target reduced the largest winning trade from $7510 to $3900, but at the same time did not reduce the overall total net profit.

Table 3.4: How additional exits change the result of the LUXOR system; change of trading figures of the system tested on British pound/US dollar (FOREX), with one exit added after another, 30 minute bars, 21/10/2002-4/7/2008, with entry time window 9.30am-1.30pm GMT. SLOW=44, FAST=1. Including $30 S+C per RT.

	Without Exit	With Stop Loss 0.3%	With Stop loss 0.3% and Trail Stop 0.8%	With Stop loss 0.3% and Trail Stop 0.8% and Profit Target 1.9%
Total Net Profit	$115,502	$116,209	$126,772	$132,590
Gross Profit	$428,864	$399,440	$405,347	$414,533
Gross Loss	($313,362)	($283,232)	($278,576)	($281,944)
Profit Factor	1.37	1.41	1.46	1.47
Total Number of Trades	902	1025	1040	1051
Percent Profitable	42.02%	34.34%	35.38%	35.20%
Winning Trades	379	352	368	370
Losing Trades	523	673	672	681
Avg. Trade Net Profit	$128	$113	$122	$126
Avg. Winning Trade	$1,132	$1,135	$1,101	$1,120
Avg. Losing Trade	($599)	($421)	($415)	($414)
Ratio Avg. Win:Avg. Loss	1.89	2.7	2.66	2.71
Largest Winning Trade	$6,748	$6,748	$7,510	$3,900
Largest Losing Trade	($2,531)	($810)	($810)	($810)
Max. Consecutive Winning Trades	6	5	6	6
Max. Consecutive Losing Trades	13	12	12	12
Avg. Bars in Total Trades	78.82	52.81	49.47	46.79
Avg. Bars in Winning Trades	116.73	108.74	100.75	93.42
Avg. Bars in Losing Trades	51.34	23.56	21.39	21.45
Percent of Time in the Market	99.92%	73.56%	69.98%	66.70%
Max. Drawdown (Intraday Peak to Valley)	($18,894)	($11,266)	($10,292)	($10,292)
Date of Max. Drawdown	24-May-06	24-Feb-06	24-Feb-06	24-Feb-06
Total Slippage and Commission	$27,060	$30,750	$31,200	$31,530

Left column: system without exits

Second column: system with 0.3% risk stop loss

Third column: system with 0.3% risk stop and a 0.8% trailing stop

Right column: system with 0.3% risk stop, 0.8% trailing stop and 1.9% profit target

How exits are affected by money management

The risk and money management of a trading system or of a whole portfolio of systems and markets can never be separated completely. The two components are highly dependent on each other. Therefore it is essential that your money management strategy is integrated into an overall approach to system design and development. Money management does not exist in a vacuum but is based on proper pre-calculated exits within your applied risk management schemes for every single trading system. In this section we will show the interplay of the two components on the practical example of our trend-following trading system LUXOR.

Figure 3.19: Scatter graph of profits for all generated trades of the LUXOR system. Tested on British pound/US dollar (FOREX), 30 minute bars, 21/10/2002-4/7/2008, with entry time window 9.30am-1.30pm GMT. SLOW=44, FAST=1. Including $30 S+C per RT.
A: without added exits. B: with 0.3% risk stop loss (red line), 1.9% profit target (green line) and 0.8% trailing stop. The exits act like borders for the trade distribution. Graphs created with TradeStation 8.

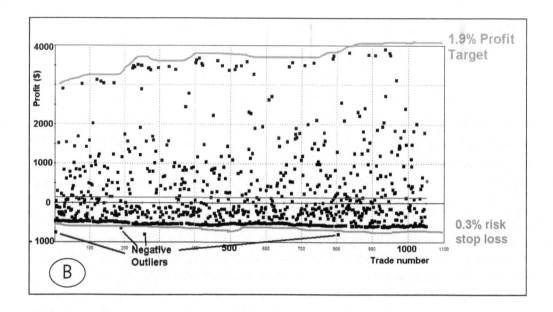

Figure 3.19 shows the profits and losses of all generated trades of the system. Whereas in Figure 3.19A you see the result of the trading system without added exits, Figure 3.19B shows the trades with the following exits in place: a profit target of 1.9%, a risk stop loss of 0.3% and a trailing stop of 0.8%.

In contrast to the MAE/MFE graphs the scatter graphs show on the horizontal axis just the number of each trade. There is no more display of any drawdowns or run-ups that a trade has had within its lifetime. We start here with this simpler demonstration since it can show more clearly the effects of the applied exits. When you compare the scatter graphs of the generated trades without and with exits some interesting impacts of the exits become apparent.

The first point is that the difference between the biggest winning trades and the biggest losing trades becomes smaller with added exits. Whereas without any exits the trades are widespread between losses of over $2000 and gains of over $6000 they are pressed closer together by applied profit target and stops to an interval between about -$500 (largest losses) and $4000 (largest gains). The dark cloud of trades which somehow looks like a swarm of bees seems now to be captured between the ground (stop loss) and a roof (profit target). The two borders are not straight lines since we are using percentage based exits instead of fixed dollar exits. These dynamic types of exits adapt themselves to the point value of the traded British pound/US dollar market.

Concerning the stop loss you can see that not all of the trades near this line are really situated between the 1.9% profit target and the 0.3% stop loss. Four negative outliers lead to higher losses than the pre-calculated 0.3% since the stop loss is sometimes over-rolled by occurring gaps. As mentioned above the biggest losing trade is therefore about 0.4% ($810) instead of 0.3% ($600). Keep in mind that in the reality of trading, especially when dealing with higher lots in non-liquid markets, bigger losses than your pre-calculated ones can always happen. They will not harm you much, however, if you consider them in advance and if your trading system is stable enough to produce the results which you have calculated nearly 100% of the time – like in the case we show here.

In contrast to the permeable behaviour of the initial stop loss you find no trades above the 1.9% target line. Because the target is chosen very far away from the entry point only few trades are able to reach it and no trade manages to pass it by using a market gap. So the scatter graphs show the effects of the 0.3% risk stop loss and the 1.9% profit target.

But what about the 0.8% trailing stop which is also in place? Whereas the primitive scatter graphs do not show the effect of the trailing stop, it can be made visible in the MFE diagram (Figure 3.20). The MFE scatter graph shows how the trailing stop (marked blue) affects both some of the losing trades (red points, left side) and some of the winning trades (right side). The trailing stop follows trades which have a big run-up and pulls the stop with a distance of 0.8% behind them in order to keep their profits. The diagram shows that this stop is very effective in most cases and was only over-rolled by a negative outlier trade in one case. On the left side of the MFE graphic you see again the effect of the risk stop loss with the four outliers mentioned above.

Figure 3.20: How the Exits prepare for Money Management. MFE diagram of all trades. How risk stop loss and trailing stops affect the trade distribution and make trades more calculable. Graph created with TradeStation 8.

The added exits make the risks of the LUXOR trading system more calculable. Although you do not know if the initiated position will be a winning or a losing trade, after having added the exits you know that it is very likely in the area between a 0.3% loss and a 1.9% win. You cannot tell this for sure, since there are some outlier trades which cannot always be stopped by your exits exactly at the pre-calculated values, but you can have fairly high confidence. This knowledge is useful in order to determine how much money you can spend on the next trade if you want to risk a certain percentage of your trading capital. This is an important step in order to apply a money management scheme which helps you to enhance your returns (see Chapter 7).

3.6 Summary: Step-by-step development of a trading system

In this chapter we have shown in the example of the GBP/USD currency pair how to develop a new trading system step-by-step (Figure 3.21). Every trading system starts with an idea and a sound logic. The idea for our trading system LUXOR was taken from the STAD TradeStation Development Club but there are many other good sources of ideas including books, the internet and seminars. Once you have found the idea, you have to test it and change it according to your needs. Therefore you should somehow transfer the idea into an algorithm, a sequence of rules, which you can apply to historic market data. During this test process you will find new ideas and you will face new problems, e.g. how to program your code correctly and how to handle weak points of your software.

Although this process is time-consuming it is valuable since you get a very detailed knowledge of your trading system. This knowledge is a key factor for your success when applying your system, since confidence and trust in your trading system is the most important factor. If you don't trust your system, you will stop trading it when the first drawdown occurs. So all the tests – with and without slippage and commissions, with and without exits, with optimisations and stability tests – are later rewarded with a good expertise about what you are doing and why you are doing it. In this way you come up with a trading system that contains a reliable risk management and prepares you for money management since you get a better estimation of the outcome of the trades.

Figure 3.21: Step-by-step development of a trading system. From an idea to a final system including entries, exits, trading costs etc.

4

Two methods for evaluating the system's predictive power

'Once you have a system, the biggest obstacle is trusting it.'
Tom Wills

In order to check the robustness of the LUXOR trading system we now perform the following two reliability tests.

4.1 Timescale analysis. We keep the system's input parameters unchanged while we change the bar length of the tested market.

4.2 Monte Carlo analysis. Changing the order of the performed trades gives you valuable estimations about expected maximum drawdowns.

Whereas Monte Carlo analysis is a well-known tool for anyone who has had experience with the evaluation of risks, timescale analysis is a new method which we have not seen in any publications so far. We find it a useful tool which can be easily performed with any standard software package that allows the bar compression of the used price data to be changed.

4.1 Timescale analysis

Changing the compression of the price data

In order to perform a test we need to have data that was not used during the building and the development of the trading system. This data is called out-of-sample data. The simplest way to get such out-of-sample data for your trading system is just apply it to the same market and the same data but to change the timescale. Although in this way the new timescale is not really different, its price structure changes a lot within diverse timescales. Therefore many valuable trading systems which work well on one timescale fail completely on another scale in the same market.

As far as the trading system LUXOR is concerned, for timescale analysis, you first develop and test a trading system step-by-step on one timescale, like we did on 30 minute data. You develop the entries, you add trading costs, then through optimisation and filtering you will arrive at a complete system with stops and profit targets. Then you just take this whole trading system and apply it like it is to the same market on different timescales. With today's software platforms like TradeStation 8 such system tests can be performed very easily.

You keep all your applied strategies on the chart while changing the symbol properties: in this case you are changing the bar length from 30 minute to any other, for example 5 minute, 10 minute, 120 minute, daily etc. If you perform such a change you see that the chart and the indicators which you use for signal generation look very similar, although you are working on different timescales (Figure 4.1). Since the indicators, in our case the two moving averages, are calculated on the basis of the chart bars, it does not matter very much if the bars are calculated every 5 minutes, 30 minutes or 120 minutes. But although the properties of some indicators look similar, the market in fact behaves very differently when looking at its different timescales in more detail. Keep in mind that on the 5 minute scale you watch the price data over 5 years much more closely than on larger timescales like the 120 minute timeframe.

Whereas in the 120 minute timescale 120 bars mean half a month of price data, the same amount of bars on a 5 minute timescale just contains half a day (Figure 4.1).

Figure 4.1 British pound/US dollar FOREX on different timescales: A: 5 minute bars, B: 30 minute bars, C: 120 minute bars. Chart examples from July 2008. The two moving averages like all other parameters for signal generation are kept the same while changing the timescale of the chart. Each of the three figures shows about 100-150 bars.

LUXOR tested on different bar compressions

It is fascinating to check how a trading strategy changes on different timescales regarding its important system figures and equity lines. Let's do such a timescale analysis for the LUXOR trading system. As you remember LUXOR was developed on 30 minute data of the British pound/US dollar FOREX market. Let's have a look at the equity lines on different timescales (Figure 4.2). You see from these curves that our developed system logic gains steady profits on all the different timescales, starting from 5 minute up to 180 minute bar calculations.

Figure 4.2 Detailed equity curves from system tests on different timescales – from 5 minute up to 180 minute bar calculations. Trend-following system British pound/US dollar (FOREX), 30 minute bars, 21/10/2002-4/7/2008, with entry time window 9.30am-1.30pm GMT. SLOW=44, FAST=1. All three exits in place: 0.3% risk stop, 0.8 trailing stop and 1.9% profit target. Including $30 S+C per RT.

Although the trading system makes profits on all the different timescales, the shapes of the equity curves with their drawdown phases appear a bit different.

Net profit and maximum drawdown dependent on the traded bar length

We'll now have a closer look at the trading system's behaviour by comparing important trading figures as a function of the chosen bar lengths.

When plotting the total net profit and the maximum intraday drawdown of the trading system for the test period as a function of the chosen timescale some interesting features are revealed (Figure 4.3). You see a very broad region of bar lengths between 5 and 35 minutes which all produce relatively similar good returns with similar low drawdowns. The 30 minute timescale is the most profitable but it is well placed in an area of other useful timescales. However, you should pay attention to the fact that at about 40 minutes the profit decreases quite a lot. As a consequence of this graph it could be even safer to use the LUXOR system on smaller timeframes like 20 minutes or 25 minutes where you also have good results but you are further away from the less profitable timescales. As you can see when you go down to very small timescales, like 1 minute bars, the system is not profitable any more. For larger timescales above the most profitable region of 5-35 minute bars the gained total net profit goes further and further down until it diminishes completely for bar lengths above 210 minutes.

Figure 4.3: Timescale analysis. Total net profit and maximum drawdown as a function of the bar length. Trend-following system British pound/US dollar (FOREX), 30 minute bars, 21/10/2002-4/7/2008, with entry time window 9.30am- 1.30pm GMT. SLOW=44, FAST=1. All three exits in place: 0.3% risk stop, 0.8 trailing stop and 1.9% profit target. Including $30 S+C per RT.

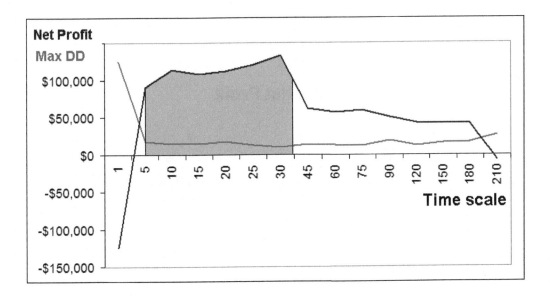

Explanation for the time dependency of the system

What are the reasons for the system's total net profit time dependency?

To understand this you need to remind yourself that the total net profit of a trading system is the number of all trades multiplied with the average profit per trade (Figure 4.4). For example let's say that you have a trading system which generates 1000 trades. In this case an average profit per trade of $100 leads to a total net profit of $100,000 (1000 x $100).

Figure 4.4: The total net profit of a trading system is the product of two factors: number of trades and average profit per trade.

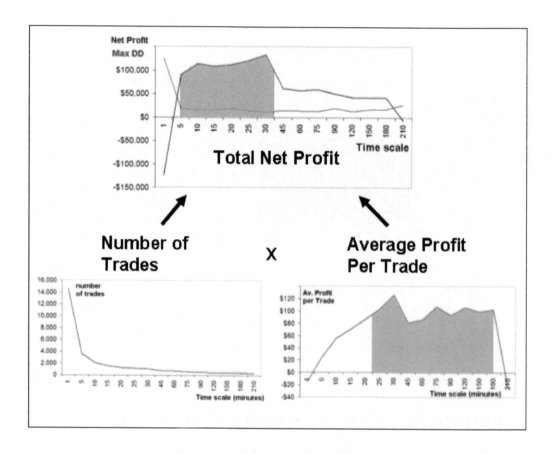

Therefore to understand the total net profit of a trading system, you must investigate the two factors which contribute to it: number of trades and average profit per trade. If you first look at the number of trades which are generated within the test period 2002-2008 you see that it strongly depends on the selected timeframe (Figure 4.5). The smaller you set the timeframe, the higher is the number of generated trades. On a 1 minute scale our trading logic generates over 14,000 trades in the 5 years whereas on a 210 minute basis only 210 trades are generated. In other words: on a 1 minute basis you get more than 2000 trades per year or 10 trades per day whereas on a 120 minute basis you only get about 40 trades per year, which means about one per week. This is plausible because on a smaller time scale you have many more bars for calculation, as discussed above (see Figure 4.1).

Figure 4.5: Timescale analysis. Number of generated trades as a function of the bar length. Trend-following system British pound/US dollar (FOREX), 30 minute bars, 21/10/2002-4/7/2008, with entry time window 9.30am-1.30pm GMT. SLOW=44, FAST=1. All three exits in place: 0.3% risk stop, 0.8 trailing stop and 1.9% profit target. Including $30 S+C per RT.

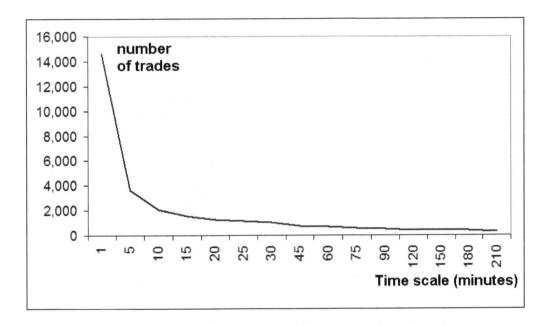

Let's look at the second factor in the calculation of total net profit; the average profit per trade as a function of the selected timescale (Figure 4.6). You see that the smaller the timescale chosen, the smaller the profit per trade you get. The worst situation appears on the 1 minute timescale, where the profit per trade becomes negative. It seems that the statistical noise is too high within the very small timescales of 1 minute to 5 minute bars. Too many arbitrary movements take place there which are difficult to exploit systematically with our trading system. Furthermore, trading costs and slippage matter more on the very small timescales. If you stay away from the very small bar lengths and set them to values between 25 and 180 minutes then the system produces an average profit per trade between $80 and $120 (green area in Figure 4.6). This is really a remarkable result since you have to keep in mind how much the market structure changes when varying the timescale in this big range.

Figure 4.6: Timescale analysis. Average profit per trade as a function of the bar length. Trend-following system British pound/US dollar (FOREX), 30 minute bars, 21/10/2002-4/7/2008, with entry time window 9.30am-1.30pm GMT. SLOW=44, FAST=1. All three exits in place: 0.3% risk stop, 0.8 trailing stop and 1.9% profit target. Including $30 S+C per RT.

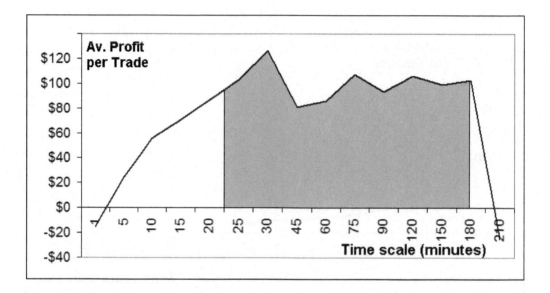

From the variation of the total number of trades and average profit per trade depending on the selected bar length you can conclude how the total net profit varies with changing timescale. On the very short timescales the total net profit suffers from a too low profit per trade. But already with timescales longer than 5 minutes the low average profit per trade can be compensated with the higher number of trades and leads the trading system to a high total net profit with low maximum drawdown. If you increase the timescale further, above 40 minutes and more, the total net profit becomes lower and lower since less and less trades are generated while the single trade profit does not increase. As a consequence our trading system works best in the medium timescales between 10 and 35 minutes.

Now what do all these findings mean for the predictive power of our trading system? The trading system which was developed and optimised on the 30 minute timescale shows promising results under variation of the timescale. From these results with the proven stability you can draw the conclusion that the trading logic has a good chance of standing up to further out-of-sample data tests and can be profitable in real trading.

4.2 Monte Carlo analysis

'What is the last thing you do before you climb on a ladder? You shake it. And that is Monte Carlo simulation.'

Sam Savage, Stanford University [10]

Nearly everybody has heard of it, but nobody uses it. Many people are afraid that Monte Carlo analysis is such a complex method that in order to understand it you must be a professor in mathematics. However the truth is that it is not that difficult and it should be used by everybody who wants to do more than just to look at the gained equity lines of system back-tests.

The principle of Monte Carlo analysis

But what does Sam Savage mean when he says that Monte Carlo analysis is just a technique to shake a ladder before climbing on it? To understand his sentence you first must know what the ladder is and what can be shaken on it.

As you probably assume, in our case the ladder is a trading system. Figure 4.7 shows this ladder, the detailed equity curve of the trading system LUXOR, with all filters and exits applied as explained in Chapter 3.

Figure 4.7: Detailed Equity Curve of system LUXOR. Tested on British pound/US dollar (FOREX), 30 minute bars, 21/10/2002-4/7/2008. With entry time window 9.30am-1.30pm GMT. SLOW=44, FAST=1. All three exits in place: 0.3% risk stop, 0.8% trailing stop and 1.9% profit target. Including $30 S+C per RT. Calculation based on one contract basis, results incl. $30 slippage and commissions per trade. Chart created with Market System Analyzer (see www.adaptrade.com).

This detailed equity curve represents all the 1051 trades performed by the trading system within the test period 21/10/2002-4/7/2008, one after another in a chronological order.

Now let's shake the ladder as following: you keep all these 1051 trades (e.g. trade 1=$120 win, trade 2=$90 loss, trade 3=$445 win … trade 1051=$150 loss) and you put them into a new order. Figure 4.8 shows an example of how you do this with a trading system that contains six trades: each of the six trades is kept but put into a new position.

Figure 4.8: The principle of Monte Carlo analysis: A trading system which contains six trades is "shaken" – this means that the positions of the six trades are exchanged accidentally.

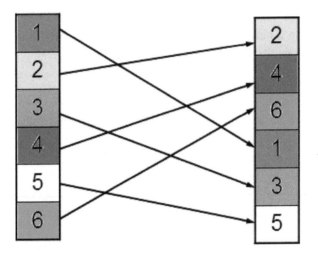

You can do it in the same way with every arbitrary number of trades. The new positions of the trades are determined randomly. For example, in our system trade 1 is now in position 842, trade 2 in position 66, trade 1051 in position 980 etc. The important point is that every trade still exists like before – no trade is deleted and no trade is added. This permutation method is called "selection without replacement"[4].

---

[4] Another possible permutation method is selection with replacement. The advantage of a selection without replacement is that it exactly duplicates the probability distribution of the input sequence, whereas selection with replacement may not. The drawback to selection without replacement is that the randomly sampled trade sequences are limited to the number of trades in the input sequence. Thus if you have a short sequence of trades (e.g. less than 50 trades), this may limit the accuracy of your calculations. The first method is similar to random selection with replacement with the advantage that the final list of trades will have the same statistical properties as the original list. The second method introduces more randomness into the trade sequence, which may be preferable if the expected trades in the future will likely be different than those of the original sequence.

Exchanging the order of the performed trades

The above example suggests that the final outcome of all trades must stay the same, independent of whatever new order the trades are placed in. Since the sum of your trades stays the same all new equity curves must reach the same amount in the end. But since the trades are now in a new order, the shape of the new equity lines and especially the occurring drawdowns become different (Figure 4.9).

Figure 4.9: Blue: detailed equity curve, Black: 15 permutations of the trades sequence ("shaken trades"). Trend-following system LUXOR British pound/US dollar (FOREX), 30 minute bars, 21/10/2002-4/7/2008. Calculation based on one contract basis, results including $30 slippage and commissions per trade.

This figure shows the original trade sequence (thick blue line) and 15 permuted trade sequences (thin black lines). All the permutated equity curves have the same starting and ending points because we did not add or remove any trades but just changed the order of their appearance. The change of the trade orders leads to the effect that between the equity curves there are big variations with different drawdown phases that occur at different times.

Probabilities and confidence levels

Now that you have grasped how your trading system can be shaken we need to bring ahead the understanding of Monte Carlo analysis just one step further. You can do this sampling not only 15 times but many more times. In fact with 1051 different trades you have 1051! = 1051*1050*1049*1048*...*3*2*1 possible permutations, an unbelievable high number[5]! Bear in mind that even the apparently small number of 200! (200*199*198...*3*2*1) is bigger than the number of all the atoms that exist in the complete universe! The job of calculating all these different possibilities cannot even be done by fast computers within a reasonable time. For these practical reasons in Monte Carlo analysis you chose "only" some hundreds or thousands of such arbitrary trade sequences randomly. The results are sorted and from this classified list probabilities for each result can be assigned. The following simple example will demonstrate how to determine such probabilities:

Consider flipping a coin 1000 times and estimating the amounts of heads and tails. If the coin is built completely symmetrically (which is not possible in real life but used by mathematicians who do statistical calculations) then you can call this coin "fair". While it is likely that the number of heads and tails with such a fair coin will be close to 500, it is also unlikely that they will both be exactly 500. What is far more likely is that the number of heads will fall in some range around 500. Instead of getting a head exactly 500 times and tails exactly 500 times you get a Gaussian distribution of values around 500 (Figure 4.10). This leads us to the introduction of a so called "confidence level" and "confidence interval".

These values describe the distribution of the experimentally gained data around the true parameter (in this case 500). The confidence level (95%) says how likely it is that the true parameter of 500 is placed within the confidence interval around your estimation. For the Gaussian distribution, which is applicable for this ideal experiment, you can be 95% sure that the value 500 is accurate within 3.1%. This means that with 95% probability you will throw between 469 (500 times -3.1%) and 531 times (500 times +3.1%) a head from the 1000 trials.

---

[5] The first trade you can put on 1051 different positions, the second trade has 1050 positions left, the third trade 1049 positions and so on: 1051*1050*...*2*1 possibilities.

Figure 4.10: Gaussian distribution of probabilities for flipping a coin 1000 times. You can tell with 95% confidence that the coin falls to heads between 469 and 531 times. Figure created with MATLAB.

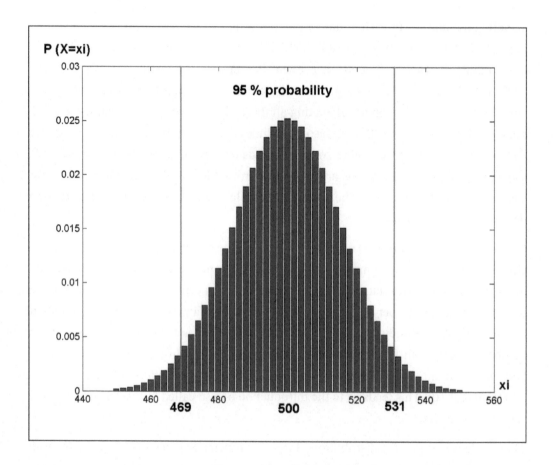

These confidence levels (e.g. 95%, 99% confidence etc) are used in Monte Carlo analysis.

Performing a Monte Carlo analysis with the LUXOR trading system

Let's look at the concrete example of a Monte Carlo analysis of our trading system LUXOR (Table 4.1).

Table 4.1: Monte Carlo analysis of 5000 permutations with worst case maximum drawdown and average drawdown as a function of confidence level. Trend-following system LUXOR British pound/US dollar (FOREX), 30 minute bars, 21/10/2002-4/7/2008. Calculation based on one contract basis, results including $30 slippage and commissions per trade. Calculation performed with Market System Analyzer.

Test period:	21/10/2002-4/7/2008	
Market	GBP/USD, 30 min bars	
Costs:	30$ Slipp. + Comm.	
Number of samples for Monte Carlo Analysis	5000	
Total Net Profit	$132,589.50	
Final Account Equity	$142,589.50	
Total Number of Trades	1,051	
Number of Winning Trades	370	
Number of Losing Trades	681	
Largest Winning Trade	$3,900.00	
Average Winning Trade	$1,120.36	
Largest Losing Trade	($810.00)	
Average Losing Trade	($414.01)	
	Worst Case Max. Drawdown	**Worst Case Average Drawdown**
ORIGINAL SYSTEM	($10,292)	($1,976)
MONTE CARLO results at 60% confidence	($12,321)	($2,006)
MONTE CARLO results at 70% confidence	($13,222)	($2,040)
MONTE CARLO results at 80% confidence	($14,325)	($2,090)
MONTE CARLO results at 90% confidence	($16,136)	($2,176)
MONTE CARLO results at 95% confidence	($17,908)	($2,259)
MONTE CARLO results at 99% confidence	($21,364)	($2,308)

Looking at the top of the table you see that most of the trading system figures stay the same for all different confidence levels. This is clear from our above discussions. During the performed type of Monte Carlo analysis you just change the order of the trades when shaking them but you do not cancel or add any trades since in our case we chose the method "selection without replacement". So most of the trading figures like average trade, total net profit, total number of trades, final account equity, biggest winning trade, biggest losing trade, average winning trade etc stay the same when you perform your 5000 permutations.

The most important aspect of Monte Carlo analysis is the estimation of expected drawdowns. The Monte Carlo analysis is a tool which checks for possible worst case scenarios. It looks for the worst drawdowns which can happen in the lifetime of your trading logic. In our case the trading system has a maximum drawdown of $10,292 and an average drawdown of $1976 (Table 4.1). The performed Monte Carlo analysis tells you, with 99% confidence, that the worst case drawdown of our trading system will not exceed $21,364 and usually average drawdowns will be in the range around $2000. So by bringing all trades into different order 5000 times with 99% confidence the worst case drawdown will not become bigger than $21,364.

Although this number is more than double the drawdown of the original system, $21,364 maximum expected drawdown is not more than the average profit per year ($22,000 = $132,000/6 years). This value is acceptable for a single trading system. But still our calculation means that if you start the system for the first time you have to be prepared that there is a 1% chance of facing a $21,000 drawdown before making any profits. Keep in mind that 99% confidence is a quite high level. If you look at lower confidence levels, your expected worst-case drawdowns and average drawdowns get remarkably lower.

Limitations of the Monte Carlo method

If you want to estimate the real risks which are hidden below the results of your performance table, Monte Carlo analysis is the right method. But when drawing conclusions from Monte Carlo calculations you still must keep in mind the assumptions on which they are based and their limitations. The dangerous point is that for the Monte Carlo analysis you take the trades from the trading logic as you get them from your back-tests. But what if this trading logic is only curve fitted and over-optimised? The Monte Carlo analysis cannot see this! Since it just takes the trades of your system (which might be over-fitted) it usually shows a good result if the back-test is good. On the other side it shows bad results only if the back-test is bad.

So Monte Carlo analysis is only useful when applied correctly and not to over-fitted trading systems. And still, even if it is applied correctly, you need to be careful in its interpretation. Sometimes things on the markets take place which cannot be avoided:

> And some events are beyond the model's ability to predict them. The brainy sorts at Long-Term Capital Management, the hedge fund that imploded during 1998, employed sophisticated probability models. But those models failed dramatically during a financial calamity that was triggered by a default in Russia. That's a warning that this high-tech planning is not foolproof. My concern is that people are using Monte Carlo as a certainty test. It isn't. It's a probability test. [10]

A decade later we know that the crisis in 1998 was very small compared to what is just starting to happen now and could not be predicted by any mathematical models.

Keep in mind that in Monte Carlo analysis the following assumption is used: returns of markets follow a Gaussian, normal distribution like the perfect flipping coin (Figure 4.10). However the reality in the financial markets is different! Figure 4.11 shows the daily changes of the British pound in US dollars within the last twenty years. Although the general behaviour of the markets can be described by the Gauss model, there are some days with very huge percentage changes that are outside the Gaussian curve.

Such days are impossible to predict and the Monte Carlo analysis which is based on the Gaussian distribution reaches its limits. To get more reliable results for such extreme scenarios you have to choose more realistic distributions than the Gaussian distribution, leading to more complex mathematical models which go beyond the scope of this book.

Figure 4.11: Daily changes of the British pound vs. US dollar in percent from August 1988-August 2008. Biggest gain was 2.8%, biggest loss 3.3%. The Gaussian distribution cannot describe the daily changes exactly, especially for large gains and losses (encircled areas). Figure generated with MATLAB, data taken from TradeStation 8.

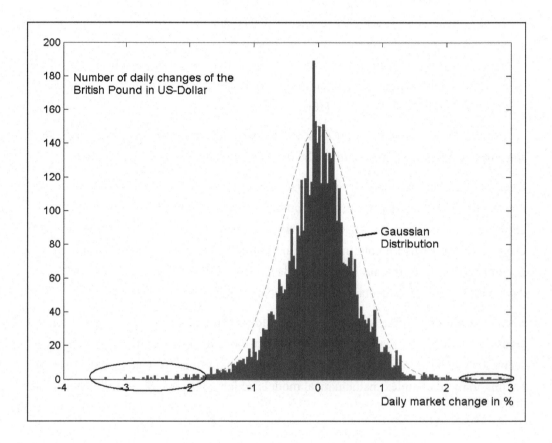

5

The factors around your system

Many traders believe that the system code is what counts in becoming a successful trader. In fact the code is the **least** important thing since there are many other factors around a trading system. These factors are discussed in this chapter.

If you are a systematic trader you have probably already had the following experience. You develop a trading system by accident after some time-consuming research. Its back-test results look promising and its logic seems sound. You decide to start to trade it but the real performance is not as good as you expected. Your trading system still contains a slight upward bias in real trading but it is far away from the bright results which your tests showed. Why does this happen? Are there any ways to avoid this and to be sure that the back-test results will hold in real trading? Although we do not want to arrive at a final answer to these questions in this chapter we will try to pinpoint the main traits of this topic. The argument is complex and unfortunately there is no room for a short and easy formula that the reader can adhere to without leaving a critical standpoint. We focus therefore on the question of how much predictive power your trading system needs to have for the future and we try to find out which factors the trading system's predictive power depends on.

Most of the theoretic base of this work is provided by David Aronson's book, *Evidenced-Based Technical Analysis* [2]. We take it here as our main reference and we will look at the topic from a practical point of view with real examples of trading systems.

5.1 The market's long/short bias

When developing trading systems the market "mood" is a key factor. It is very different if the market under scrutiny was in an upward, sideways or downward trend within the test period. In the bull market 1995-2000 many trading systems performed the best on the stock markets and futures like FTSE 100, S&P 500, Nasdaq etc. which had a long bias. When the market turned down after 2001 these systems went bust. While they had been able to gain huge profits between 1997 and 2000 they met harsh difficulties during the bear market in the afterwards years.

The trend is your friend?

We'll discuss this so called long/short bias of a market here on the example of the British pound/US dollar FOREX (Figure 5.1). As you can see the market shows an overall upward trend in the test period. Whereas the pound was trading at $1.50 six years ago, it became very strong against the dollar within the last five years and in summer 2008 traded at around $2. If you now develop a trading system which goes long in the year 2002 and stays long until July 2008 you will have earned more than $50,000 with one contract (Figure 5.2). But as you can see the trading equity (= the gained money) of this simple system behaves exactly the same as the traded market itself.

As you can imagine every only-long trading system with a similar result to this is almost useless. Since the market itself has an upward bias it is no big achievement of an only-long trading system to gain money. On the other hand every system which enters only on the short side and has not lost any money within the test period 2002-2008 can be a useful trading logic for the future. It will probably earn money as soon as the market goes sideways or even reverses into a downward trend.

As you see from the underwater equity curve (Figure 5.2B) the only-long system, although it has good returns, is very risky. It stays in the market 100% of the time and therefore suffers huge drawdowns. Moreover the system needs nearly two years to recover from its biggest losing period.

Figure 5.1: British pound/US dollar (FOREX), weekly bars, 1/7/2002-4/7/2008. A long entry signal is placed on 21/10/2002.

Figure 5.2: Only long trading system for British pound/ US dollar (FOREX), 1/7/2002-4/7/2008. A long entry signal is placed on 21/10/2002 and the system stays in the market all the time. A: detailed equity curve; B: underwater equity curve showing all drawdowns.

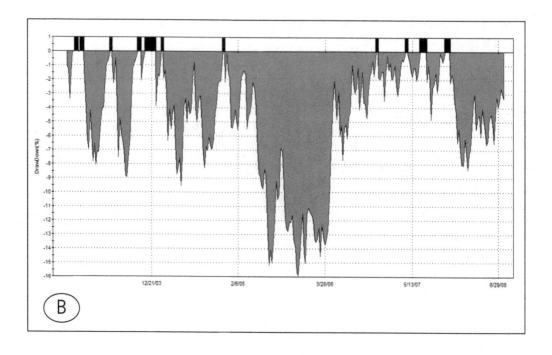

Consequences for system development

When developing a trading system you can compare its long side with this only-long system, as the minimum result to achieve. You know how much of the profit was earned simply by the market trend and the additional achievement of your trading logic compared with this market bias. The most important figure of your system tests is thereby the total percentage of time your trading system has been in the market. Only if the system was in the market 100% of time is the market bias 100% important. If you trade, however, a system which is only very seldom in the market, let's say only 10%, the market bias becomes less important. Another reason to keep the time in the market low is to decrease the risk and exposure as discussed in Chapter 3.5 when we talked about exits and risk management.

What other conclusions can you draw as a systematic trader or system developer from the long/short bias of markets? When you look at the trading systems which we present here you can see that most of them have a similar amount of short and long trades. Although in some cases (stocks and stock index futures) markets crash more quickly than they go upwards, we tend to build the systems without long or short bias. Most of our systems (like LUXOR) have a similar amount of long and short trades, although their profitability in a long or short direction may be different because the market has shown an uptrend. Since you do not know if this uptrend will continue in the future, your system is more stable and less adapted to this market bias if it produces the same amount of long and short signals.

5.2 Out-of-sample deterioration

David Aronson stated a fact which we absolutely agree with from our own experience in systems' evaluation [2]:

> Market behaviour is presumed to be a combination of systematic behaviour (recurring patterns) and random noise. It is always possible to improve the fit of a rule to a given segment of data by increasing its complexity. In other words, given enough complexity, it is always possible to fashion a rule that buys at every market low point and sells at every market high point. This is a bad idea. Perfect timing on past data can only be the result of a rule that is contaminated with noise. In other words, perfect signals or anything approaching them almost certainly means the rule is, to a disturbing degree, a description of past random behaviour (i.e. overfitted). Overfitting is manifested when the rule is applied to the test data segment. There, its performance will be worse than in the training data. This is because the legitimate patterns found in a training set recur in the test set, but the noise in the training set does not. It can be inferred that profitability in the training set that does not repeat in the testing set was most likely a consequence of over-fitting.

This is a meaningful description of the concept of degrees of freedom as depicted more formally in Chapter 2. In this chapter we will have a look at a real example of such an over fitted system.

A Bollinger Band system with logic and code

We will stay with the pound/dollar FOREX market from 2002-2008 (Datafeed = TradeStation 8) to test the system. We take a Bollinger Band system (Figure 5.4) and optimise all its main six input parameters for the entry and exit points on daily data within the training period between 30/04/2002 and 1/3/2006 (Figure 5.3). Please note that this Bollinger Band system allows a different optimisation of its input parameters concerning the long and the short side. For the upper and the lower Bollinger Band the length of the moving averages and their distance from the entry point can be varied. So you have four input parameters which you can optimise for the entries. Furthermore we insert two variable, percentage based exits, which can be optimised as well: a risk stop loss and a profit target.

Figure 5.3: British pound/US dollar, 30/04/2002-4/7/2008. The Bollinger Band trading system is optimised in six parameters within the training data range (30/04/2002-28/02/2006). Afterwards the results of this trading system are checked in the test data range (1/3/2006-4/7/2008).

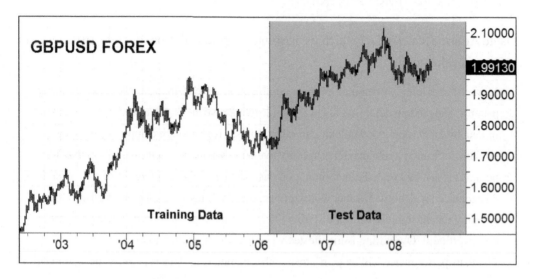

Figure 5.4A: Entry and exit logic of a Bollinger Band breakout system. Four parameters in the entry logic and two parameters in the exit logic can be optimised.

Figure 5.4B: Easy Language Code of a Bollinger Band breakout system with entry and exit logic. Four parameters in the entry logic and two parameters in the exit logic can be optimised.

Entry logic: Bollinger Band system

```
inputs:        LengthUp(18),
               NumDevsUp(2),
               LengthDn(20),
               NumDevsDn(2);


vars: UpperBand(0),
            LowerBand(0),
            Price(0);


Price = (O+H+L+C)/4 ;
//UpperBand = BollingerBand( Price, LengthUp, NumDevsUp ) ;
//LowerBand = BollingerBand( Price, LengthDn, -NumDevsDn ) ;
UpperBand = BollingerBandFC( Price, LengthUp, NumDevsUp ) ;
LowerBand = BollingerBandFC( Price, LengthDn, -NumDevsDn ) ;


if CurrentBar > 1 and High crosses under UpperBand then
      Sell Short ( "BBandSE" ) next bar at UpperBand stop ;


if CurrentBar > 1 and Low crosses over LowerBand then
      Buy ( "BBandLE" ) next bar at LowerBand stop ;


Exit Logic:


(for both long positions/short positions)

1) Place an initial stop loss x % below entry price (Opt value: x =1.9)
2) Place a profit target z % above entry price (Opt value: x =4.8)
```

Optimising the Bollinger Band system

If you optimise all these six input parameters together with an optimisation criteria focused on the highest net profit on daily data of the pound/dollar FOREX market in the period from 30/04/2002 to 28/2/2006 you get the following result (Figure 5.5).

Figure 5.5: Bollinger Band system for British pound/dollar (FOREX), daily, all six input parameters optimised for maximum total net profit, 30/04/2002-28/2/2006. A: Detailed equity curve; B: Underwater equity curve showing all drawdowns.

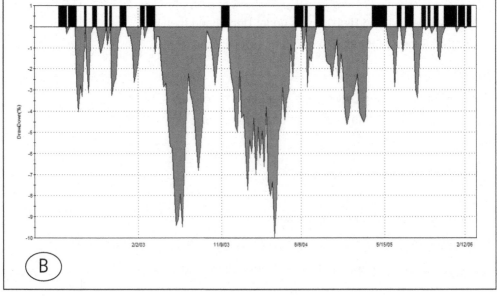

As you can see the gains of the system are steady. The drawdowns are not tiny (about 10%) but the system's profitability is high. The trading system performs nearly as many short trades as long trades and so the long/short bias of the underlying market is under control, although the trading system has high market exposure, with it holding a position in the market 89% of the time.

Out-of-sample result

Now let's see what happens if you apply the optimised trading logic to test data on which no optimisation has taken place. In this test period of two years from 1/3/2006 to 4/7/2008 you keep the same input parameters as you found in the training period (Figure 5.6).

Figure 5.6: Detailed equity curve of Bollinger Band system for British pound/ dollar (FOREX), daily, training and test period. All six input parameters optimised for maximum total net profit within the training period 30/04/2002-28/02/2006. Test period from 1/3/2006-4/7/2008.

As you can see the system has completely lost its bright performance. The smoothly increasing equity curve of the training period transformed itself into a directionless sideways movement. The steady equity curve of the training set suffers a big drawdown at the beginning of the test set, from which it needs nearly a two-year recovery period.

These obvious observations within the equity line are confirmed with the system report (Table 5.1). Whereas within the training period the system has a total net profit of $78,000, it was only $379 in the test period. From the big average profit per trade of $1131 in the training period, only $10 is left in the test period. Even the biggest intraday drawdown was worse in the small test period: $20,000 in the test period compared with $14,000 in the training period.

Table 5.1: Bollinger Band system for British pound/US dollar (FOREX), daily, training and test period. All six input parameters optimised for maximum total net profit within the training period 30/04/2002-28/2/2006. Test period from 1/3/2006-4/7/2008.

		TRAIN		TEST
Test period from		30/04/2002		01/03/2006
until		28/02/2006		04/07/2008
	All Trades		All Trades	
Total Net Profit		$78,050.50		$379.00
Gross Profit		$150,638.50		$53,000.00
Gross Loss		($72,588.00)		($52,621.00)
Profit Factor		2.08		1.01
Total Number of Trades		69		36
Total Number of Long Trades		30		16
Total Number of ShortTrades		39		20
Percent Profitable		63.77%		47.22%
Winning Trades		44		17
Losing Trades		25		19
Avg. Trade Net Profit		$1,131.17		$10.53
Avg. Winning Trade		$3,423.60		$3,117.65
Avg. Losing Trade		($2,903.52)		($2,769.53)
Ratio Avg. Win:Avg. Loss		1.18		1.13
Largest Winning Trade		$8,348.00		$6,409.00
Largest Losing Trade		($3,658.00)		($3,884.00)
Max. Consecutive Winning Trades		4		4
Max. Consecutive Losing Trades		4		6
Avg. Bars in Total Trades		13.88		15.42
Avg. Bars in Winning Trades		15.52		20.71
Avg. Bars in Losing Trades		11		10.68
Trading Period		3 Yrs, 11 Mths		2 Yrs, 4 Mths, 8 Dys
Percent of Time in the Market		89.17%		85.13%
Time in the Market		3 Yrs, 5 Mths, 27 Dys		2 Yrs, 2 Dys
Longest Flat Period		14 Dys		30 Dys
Max. Equity Run-up		$83,593.50		$19,428.00
Date of Max. Equity Run-up		28/02/2006		06/12/2007
Max. Equity Run-up as % of Initial Capital		83.59%		19.43%
Max. Drawdown (Intra-day Peak to Valley)				
Value		($14,664.00)		($20,091.00)
Date of Max. Drawdown		18/05/2004		10/08/2006

Reasons for the out-of-sample deterioration

We suggest the following reasons and discuss their possible contribution:

A: The trading logic generates less than 100 trades, therefore the results are not statistically significant.

We conducted the same experiment with the same trading system on a 30 minute basis. There the system generated 3000 trades in the training period and got a similar out-of-sample deterioration. So although 69 trades of the daily system are not enough to be statistically significant, the results shown here are typical and the low number of trades is certainly not the main reason for the system deterioration.

B: The system was published at the beginning of 2006 and the trading logic has been adopted by too many traders which destroyed its performance.

This explanation is believed by some traders who have found a new trading system or just an interesting idea. They believe that when their trading system is published the performance will suffer since other traders will immediately adopt the logic. Since many people now trade this system its good performance could diminish because of increasing slippage at first, and later because of a changing market structure since more and more people change their trading style towards the successful system. System developers try to prevent this from happening with their trading systems by hiding them in a strongbox for some years and not showing them to anybody until they lose their predictive power anyway. David Aronson writes about the topic of system disclosure in his book:

> 'This rationale also lacks plausibility. Even when numerous traders adopt similar rules, as in the case with futures trading funds that employ objective trend-following methods, reduced rule performance seems to be due to changes in market volatility that are not related to the usage of technical systems.'

In other words: although everybody knows that trend-following methods work they do still continue to work, so the disclosure of the system is not a big reason for its success or failure. Furthermore, this system has been open to the public since the day John Bollinger developed it, which was a long time before 2006.

C: The market dynamics within the training data range is different from the one in the test data range.

In our opinion this can be one part of the explanation for deterioration. We'll discuss this extensively in the next section.

D: The system has been adapted too much to market noise within the training period, i.e. curve over-fitting.

The process of optimisation favours a set of rules which fit the training data better than the test data. Let's assume that the training data, like all real market data, consists partially of recurrent patterns (predictable data) and random noise (unpredictable data). Now you take a trading system and you adapt it to this data which is partially random and partially contains a special pattern. If your trading system is simple enough but has a sound logic with valid rules, it is able to capture some parts of the recurrent predictable patterns but does not adjust itself to the market noise. In this way the trading system keeps a certain amount of predictability for the future. If you, however, add more and more rules to this system it adjusts itself more and more to the existing noise. At a certain point the system becomes over-fitted and loses its predictability for the test period, or for the future, since the noise will be different. This is probably the most important aspect of the sample deterioration and we will investigate it with a step-by-step case study in the final section of this chapter.

You can also draw another conclusion from this thesis: all artificial market data, produced with computers by random processes, only consists of noise and are therefore useless for trading system development. If you develop a trading system based on this noisy data it will have no predictive part if applied to other data showing a different type of noise. What your trading system is trying to detect are the patterns which repeat themselves. These patterns are mainly produced by human behaviour like greed, fear and exaggeration and not by random, artificial mathematical processes.

5.3 The market data bias

Expanding the training period

Now the Bollinger Band trading system is optimised within a much longer training period of daily data from 1986 to 2006 (Figure 5.7). Afterwards the results are checked within the test data range which is the same as above, from 1/3/2006 to 4/7/2008 (Figure 5.8).

As you can see, the result in the out-of-sample area (Test Set) is now positive and much better than in the test above with the optimised parameters from the short training range. A closer look at the trading figures confirms this observation (Table 5.2). You now get a total net profit of $16,757 in the test range and a good average trade net profit of nearly

$600. Please note that the average monthly return within the test range is $591, which is even higher than the average monthly return of the long test data range of $321. However the risk of this trading system is still quite high, with a maximum drawdown of $16,939. This is nearly as much as the total net profit earned in the test period. We can summarise that the result of this out-of-sample test for the Bollinger Band system with the longer training period is much better than the one which had the shorter training period.

Figure 5.7: British pound/US dollar, 03/03/1986-4/7/2008. The Bollinger Band trading system is now optimised within the long training data range 1986-2006. Afterwards the results of this trading system are checked in the test data range (green). See the shorter training range 2002-2006 which was used above.

Figure 5.8: Bollinger Band system for British pound/US dollar (FOREX), daily, training and test period. All six input parameters are now optimised for maximum total net profit within a longer training period of 20 years: 03/03/1986-28/2/2006. Test period is kept the same, from 1/3/2006-4/7/2008. A: Detailed equity curve; B: Underwater equity curve showing all drawdowns.

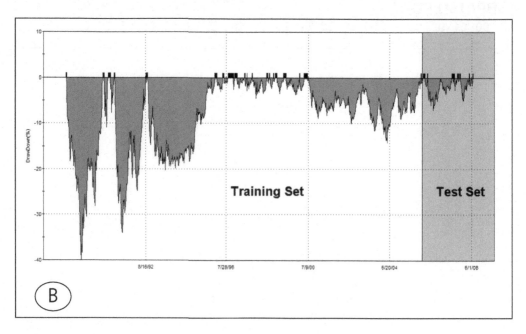

Table 5.2: Bollinger Band system for British pound/US dollar (FOREX), daily, training vs. test period. All six input parameters are now optimised for maximum total net profit within a longer training period of 20 years: 03/03/1986-28/2/2006. Test period is kept the same, from 1/3/2006-4/7/2008.

	TRAIN	TEST
Test Period from	03/03/1986	01/03/2006
until	28/02/2006	04/07/2008
Total Net Profit	$175,737.50	$16,757.00
Gross Profit	$367,121.50	$44,964.00
Gross Loss	($191,384.00)	($28,207.00)
Profit Factor	1.92	1.59
Total Number of Trades	149	28
Total Number of Long Trades	74	14
Total Number of Short Trades	75	14
Percent Profitable	63.76%	64.29%
Winning Trades	95	18
Losing Trades	52	10
Even Trades	2	0
Avg. Trade Net Profit	**$1,179.45**	**$598.46**
Avg. Winning Trade	$3,864.44	$2,498.00
Avg. Losing Trade	($3,680.46)	($2,820.70)
Ratio Avg. Win:Avg. Loss	1.05	0.89
Largest Winning Trade	$27,750.00	$5,578.00
Largest Losing Trade	($20,050.00)	($8,132.00)
Max. Consecutive Winning Trades	8	5
Max. Consecutive Losing Trades	5	3
Avg. Bars in Total Trades	34.8	22.61
Avg. Bars in Winning Trades	29.67	22.56
Avg. Bars in Losing Trades	45.42	22.7
Annual Rate of Return	5.12%	6.59%
Avg. Monthly Return	**$321.61**	**$591.59**
Std. Deviation of Monthly Return	$4,363.12	$2,723.27
Return Retracement Ratio	0.09	0.35
RINA Index	28.23	5.86
Sharpe Ratio	0.1	n/a
K-Ratio	3.3	2.12
Trading Period	19 Yrs, 11 Mths, 27 Dys	2 Yrs, 4 Mths, 4 Dys
Percent of Time in the Market	99.96%	99.42%
Time in the Market	19 Yrs, 11 Mths, 24 Dys	2 Yrs, 4 Mths, 1 Dy
Longest Flat Period	n/a	n/a
Max. Equity Run-up	$187,179.50	$29,301.00
Date of Max. Equity Run-up	28/02/2006	16/11/2007
Max. Equity Run-up as % of Initial Capital	187.18%	29.30%
Max. Drawdown (Intra-day Peak to Valley)		
Value	($39,750.00)	($16,939.00)
Date of Max. Drawdown	02/07/1991	08/08/2006

Conclusion: How to choose your training data

The results of our trading system during the test period are more similar to the results of the longer training period of 1986 to 2006 than the results of the shorter training period from 2002 to 2006. Although you cannot see this from the chart of the GBP/USD itself, the market data has a different behaviour during the different years of the test. This behaviour manifests itself in volatility, in trend duration, in a different frequency of breakouts or patterns etc, which affects the "best" parameters of the Bollinger Band system in the different training periods.

The conclusion is that it's advisable to make the training period as long as possible. Since a longer period contains much more data, there is a higher probability that within this longer data range there are some periods which behave similarly to your test data range and therefore train your system better. The longer you make the training period for your trading system the better your chances for similar results in the out-of-sample tests and later in real trading. On the other hand, keep in mind that this rule is only valid if your market data contains a lot of different market phases. If you choose a market which is always in an upward trend (like the Long Gilt from 1980 to 2000) you can train on it any trading system with a long-entry bias but it will be of no use when the market changes its bullish behaviour. If you are aware of this however, and you are careful in choosing the right training data, you can avoid having to adapt your trading system to such market biases.

5.4 Optimisation and over-fitting

Step-by-step optimisation of the LUXOR system

We now switch back to our trading system LUXOR which we presented in Chapter 3. When optimising a trading system the first point you must be sure of is that the trading logic is based on an idea which is concrete and profitable. For the trading system LUXOR we have already shown that the logic seems to be sound and profitable and additionally we have performed some stability tests with it. We now take this system and perform a step-by-step optimisation of its six input parameters. First we optimise the slow moving average, second the fast moving average, then the time window filter before we finally optimise the three applied exits one after another: risk stop loss, trailing stop and profit target (Figure 5.9).

Figure 5.9: Step-by-step optimisation of the six input parameters of the LUXOR system
1. Slow moving average, 2. Fast moving average 3. Time window filter 4. Risk stop loss 5.
Trailing stop 6. Profit target. Chart example from British pound/US dollar, 30 minute, FOREX
from 26 December 2007.

To perform our tests we again use British pound/US dollar FOREX data but we return to
the intraday 30 minute timescale. On this timescale we have nearly six years of intraday
data available, from 21/10/2002 to 4/7/2008. From the above discussion of market data
bias you know that it's advisable to use as much data for the training period as possible.
However, you must still have a big enough amount of data left for testing your strategy
out-of-sample. As a compromise we use the period from 21/10/2002 to 28/02/2007 for
training/optimisation and afterwards we check how the optimised system performs within
the subsequent test period of more than one year from 1/3/2007 to 4/7/2008.

Results depending on the number of optimised parameters

If you look at the equity lines during the training periods you can see that they improve
more and more with the optimised parameters. Starting from a directionless equity line
when no parameters are optimised the equity curve becomes more enticing as more input
parameters of the trading system are optimised. This is not surprising since the system
better adapts to the training market data the more degrees of freedom it has. Now the
main question is how the trading system behaves within the test data area, depending on
the number of optimised parameters. When no optimisation took place (i.e. the system

operated with a slow moving average based on 30 bars and a fast moving average of 10 bars, no time filter and exits in place) the result within the test data is negative (Figure 5.10A).

If you now optimise the first parameter (slow moving average set to 40) for total net profit in the training range the system result is much improved in the training region, however the equity curve of this optimised system improves only slightly in the test data range (Figure 5.10B). If you look at the trading figures (Table 5.3) you can see this result confirmed.

Table 5.3: System figures for training and test area after optimisation for total net profit of one parameter after another. The optimised values are different from the gained values in chapter 3 since the optimisation period is shorter now, not the complete data range as before.

Tested symbol:GBPUSD 30 min	TRAIN REGION: 21/10/2002-28/2/2007						
Parameter number	0	1	2	3	4	5	6
Additional optimised values	no	slow moving average=40	fast moving average=2	time window: 9:30a.m.-1:30 p.m GMT	Risk stop loss: 0.47%	trailing stop: 0.67%,	profit target: 2.25%
Total Net Profit	$17,961	$58,018	$58,449	$67,921	$80,827	$84,352	$90,240
Avg. Trade Net Profit	$12	$51	$33	$118	$127	$125	$133
Max. Drawdown (Intra-day Peak to Valley)	($18,032)	($27,644)	($14,122)	($17,884)	($12,693)	($12,199)	($12,108)
	TEST REGION: 1/3/2007-4/7/2008						
Parameter number	0	1	2	3	4	5	6
Additional optimised values	no	slow moving average=40	fast moving average=2	time window: 9:30a.m.-1:30 p.m GMT	Risk stop loss: 0.47%	trailing stop: 0.67%,	profit target: 2.25%
Total Net Profit	($12,569)	($9,736)	$18,038	$37,324	$25,062	$25,875	$25,464
Avg. Trade Net Profit	($27)	($26)	$34	$200	$126	$124	$122
Max. Drawdown (Intra-day Peak to Valley)	($16,820)	($17,613)	($8,089)	($10,097)	($8,448)	($9,970)	($9,970)

For example, the total net profit within the test data range improves only from -$12,569 to -$9,736 and the average trade from -$27 to -$26 after optimisation of the first parameter. This means practically no change. If you optimise the second important parameter for the trading system's entry, the fast moving average (to a value of 2), then you can see a further improvement within the training set. But now the improvement within the test data range is even bigger than for the training area. This is underlined with the system figures, e.g. the average trade within the test region improves from -$26 to a positive value of $34. This is even better than the value within the training region ($33).

If you now insert a third parameter into the trading system and optimise it (to a value of 9.30am-1.30pm) a dramatic change occurs. The system's results improve greatly within both the training region and the testing region. Please note, however, that the result in the test region improves more than in the training region. For example, the average profit per trade becomes $200 in the testing period against $118 in the training period. We can summarise that for the first three input parameters every optimisation of the trading system within the training period also leads to an improvement in the testing period. Sometimes the improvement in the testing period is smaller (like with parameter 1: slow moving average), sometimes it is even bigger than in the training period (like with parameter 2 and 3: fast moving average and time filter). If you now continue the optimisation of the trading system within the training period by adding suitable exits you get some really interesting findings.

Adding more optimised parameters in the training period can improve results in that area, but these additional parameters will not improve results in the testing period any more.

This out-of-sample deterioration cannot be seen directly from the equity curves (Figures 5.10C-5.10G). All equity lines keep steadily growing within the test regions with every added optimised system parameter, and drawdowns stay low. However, if you have a closer look at the system's report you see that in fact some hidden worsening takes place in the trading system (Table 5.3). The average profit per trade decreases from $200 to $126 after the optimised risk stop loss is inserted and stays in the area between $120 and $125 after inserting the next exits, trailing stop and profit target. There is similar behaviour for the maximum intraday drawdown. While the inserted risk stop loss reduces the drawdown from $10,097 to $8,448, the additional exits increase the drawdown again to nearly $10,000.

The behaviour of the trading system within the different stages of optimisation for training and test area can be seen best when you plot trading system figures against number of optimised input parameters. If you do this for the total net profit you get a good insight of what happens during the different stages of system optimisation (Figure 5.11). The figure reveals how the total net profit within the training range (blue line) steadily increases with every added optimisation parameter, whereas the performance within the test range (green line) changes with increasing system complexity. With only a few parameters being optimised the net profit in the test range increases with every additional parameter, reaching its high with the third parameter (time window filter) and then being reduced with the fourth optimised parameter (risk stop loss). It then cannot be made bigger again with further optimised parameters.

Figures 5.10 A-G: System LUXOR for British pound/US dollar (FOREX) training and test period. Training period 21/10/2002-28/2/2007 (white), test period 1/3/2007-4/7/2008 (green). One input parameter is optimised after another. A: No optimisation. B: Slow moving average: optimised value = 40. C: Fast moving average: optimised value = 2. D: Time window: optimised setting 9.30am-1.30pm GMT. E: Risk stop loss: optimised setting = 0.47% F: Trailing stop: optimised setting = 0.67%. G: Profit target: optimised setting = 2.25%. The optimised values are different from the gained values in chapter 3 since the optimisation period is shorter now, not the complete data range as before.

21/10/2002 1:30:00 PM – 04/07/2008 10:59:00 PM

21/10/2002 1:30:00 PM – 04/07/2008 10:59:00 PM

Trailing stop optimized

Training Set

Test Set

21/10/2002 1:30:00 PM – 04/07/2008 10:59:00 PM

F

Profit target optimized

Training Set

Test Set

21/10/2002 1:30:00 PM – 04/07/2008 10:59:00 PM

G

Figure 5.11: Finding an optimal rule complexity for system LUXOR for British pound/US dollar (FOREX) training and test period. The system's input parameters are optimised for maximum total net profit, from left to right, one after another, within the training period 21/10/2002-28/2/2007 (blue line = training results). Then results are checked in test data range 1/3/2007-4/7/2008 (green line = test results).

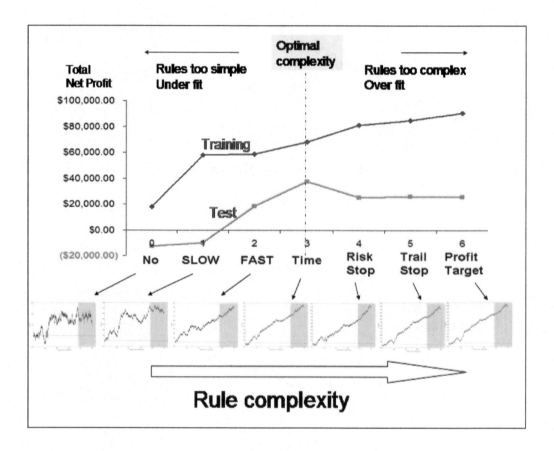

The meaning of the trading system's complexity

How can you now interpret this behaviour of the trading system?

Let's start within the diagram (Figure 5.11) from the left side when no system parameter is optimised. There the trading system has a very low complexity, since the applied rules are quite simple and not optimised at all. If you start to optimise the first parameter the system's performance changes markedly. The raw and simple trading logic used so far can easily be made better. Interestingly when not many optimised parameters have been introduced the behaviour within the test range sometimes changes more than within the training range. The change can be much worse, but it can be better than the improvement that takes place in the training range. The reason for this behaviour is that a system that has only been optimised a little reacts very sensitively to parameter changes because there are not many parameters in place yet. The rule complexity and the predictability for your test set is low.

Furthermore, keep in mind that much of what happens in different market phases and areas is accidental and also depends on the market sample bias. It can be that the out-of-sample data period is more "friendly" to our trading system logic in a certain stage than the training data period. With further parameters being optimised or added the changes in the system's reaction become smaller but still performance improves in the out-of-sample test data range. With the first three parameters being optimised our trading system reaches an important point: it reaches its optimal complexity.

From this point on every further optimised parameter (risk stop, trailing stop, profit target) decreases the system's performance in the test region although the results still improve in the training region. You now have the situation of curve over-fitting. Every new optimised parameter improves the fit of the system to the training area but what happens here is more an adjustment to the existing market noise than an improvement in predictive capability. Thus the net profit within the test region does not become bigger with further optimised parameters but instead it decreases from the fourth parameter onwards. You now again have an out-of-sample deterioration.

It should be remembered that although the results in the out-of-sample area cannot be improved any more with these exits, they still have an important function. As discussed in Chapter 3.5 when talking about risk management, every stop loss leads to a better control of risk. We see the valuable function of the stops when we look at the largest losing trades which take place in the testing region – the added stop losses decrease this figure drastically from $2,631 to $1,023 (not shown in Table 5.3). Another figure which improves with inserted exits is the time the system stays in the market, which goes down from 100% to about 80%. With exits in place the outcome of trades is more predictable and this helps you to include the trading system into a bigger portfolio and to apply position sizing methods.

5.5 Rule complexity explained with polynomial curve fitting

Interpolating data points with polynomial functions

You have just seen how a trading system's predictive power for the future changes with the number of rules which are involved in the strategy. In our system these rules have been the fast and slow moving average, the very effective intraday time filter and finally the three exits we added. You have seen that a simpler trading system has more predictive power than a more optimised one. We can state that this result was not just gained by accident but it is well founded on statistical rules. We will explain these rules now with a short discussion on interpolating data points with polynomial functions.

Let's assume that you have 10 data points as your sample data (Figure 5.12).

Figure 5.12: Ten points of sample data, generated with a sinus function and random distances from it. Curve generated with MATLAB.

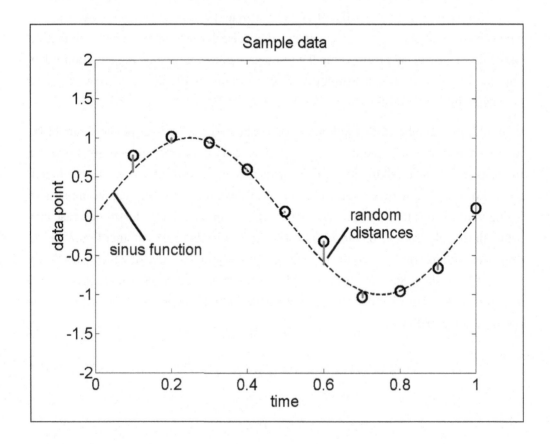

In our case the 10 points were not chosen randomly but with a combination of a rule and random behaviour. We took a sinus function which is a normal oscillation and placed the 10 points around the sinus function with randomly taken distances. Here these are just mathematical points but as a trader you can imagine that these values could also be the prices of any financial markets, for example values of a tick chart of the FTSE 100 future or any stock you like. Thus our data point simulation is an approximation for financial markets in the way that you assume that the markets have a certain order or direction (at least during special times or events) but that around this order you have lots of random behaviour and market noise.

To interpolate these 10 data points as well as possible you can use mathematic polynomial functions with different complexity. The higher the order of the polynom, the greater its complexity becomes. The easiest polynomial function (degree = 0) is a constant (Figure 5.13).

Figure 5.13: Approximation of the ten data points with a polynomial function of degree = 0, a constant with value = 0. Curve generated with MATLAB.

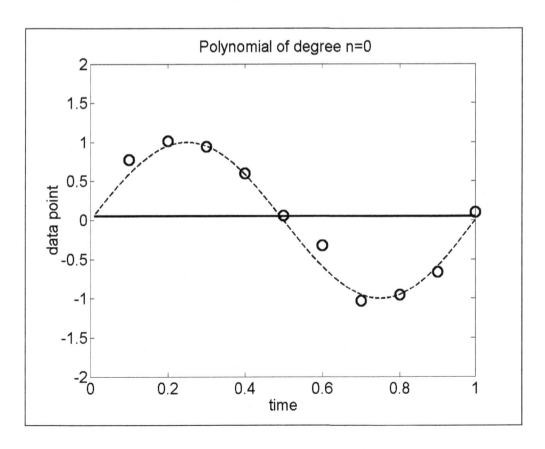

You see that this horizontal function touches some data points, but other points are a long way from it. The next higher complexity level is to interpolate the 10 data points with a linear function, which is a polynomial of degree 1 (Figure 5.14). In the picture of a trading system this line could be a simple trend line. Since the results of the constant and the linear function are rather poor fits to the 10 data points, we have to increase the adaptive function's complexity. The second order polynomial seems to give a quite good fit to the data points (Figure 5.15). This curve reaches more data points and comes quite close to all points, although not all are reached exactly. If we increase the degree of the polynomial function to 3 we already have a very nice fit to the data points and when we go to a much higher order of polynomial (degree = 9) we obtain a 100% fit to the training data (Figures 5.16 and 5.17). The polynomial of degree 9 passes exactly through each data point.

Figure 5.14: Approximation of the ten data points with a polynomial function of degree = 1, a linear function. Curve generated with MATLAB.

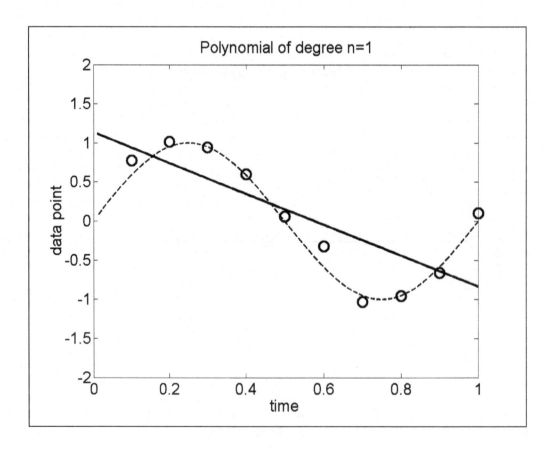

Figure 5.15: Approximation of the ten data points with a polynomial function of degree = 2, a parabolic function. Curve generated with MATLAB.

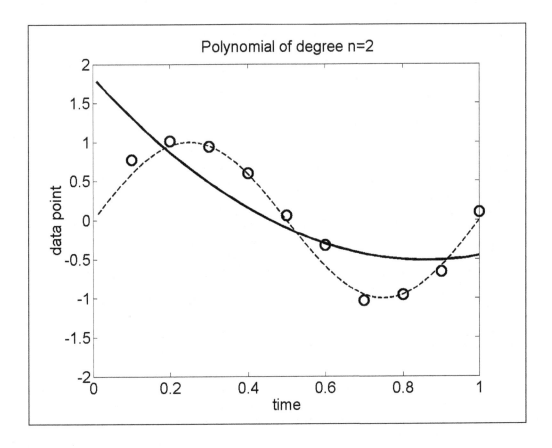

Figure 5.16: Approximation of the ten data points with a polynomial function of degree = 3. The fitness to the data points increases but also the complexity of the function. Curve generated with MATLAB.

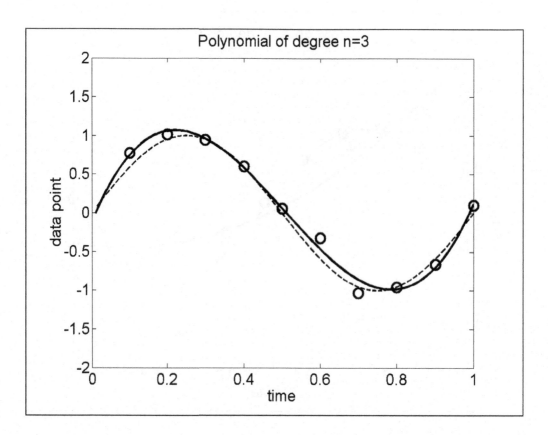

Figure 5.17: Approximation of the ten data points with a complex polynomial function of degree = 9. Curve generated with MATLAB.

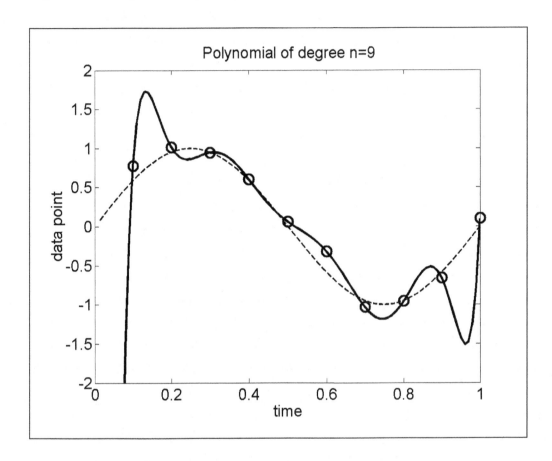

You can also plot the results of these graphs in a table (Table 5.4). There you see how the average error of the fitness function becomes smaller with a higher degree of polynomial. Whereas the polynomial of degree 0 has a big standard deviation from the 10 data points (5.39), the 9th degree polynomial nearly reaches the points without any error (0.0003).

Table 5.4: Average error of fit to data points (standard deviation) as a function of the degree of the polynomial. The higher the degree of the polynomial, the better its fit to the data points, but the higher its rule complexity becomes.

Degree of Polynomial	Average error of fit to data points (standard deviation)
0	5.3932
1	2.1863
2	1.6583
3	0.057
4	0.0555
5	0.046
6	0.0407
7	0.0407
8	0.0256
9	0.0003

If you have a closer look at the result of the 9th degree polynomial fit you can see that the fitted curve oscillates wildly and gives only a very poor representation of the chosen sinus-function with the data points randomly around it. This 9th degree polynomial could stand for a very complex trading system with many components added until you have got a perfect fit of the trading logic to your market data.

But what are the conclusions which you can draw from these fitness functions and what is the predictive power of the different polynomials for the future?

Predictive power of the different polynomials

Let's see what happens if we add further data points by letting the sinus function continue into the future (Figure 5.18). You can see that the polynomial of degree 0 continues to go sideways with the sinus function. Thus the predictive power of this very simple function for the future is quite poor, but it is worth mentioning that it stays exactly the same as the result of the back-test of the ten data points.

Figure 5.18: Predictive capability of the polynomial of degree =0 for unseen test data. Curve generated with MATLAB.

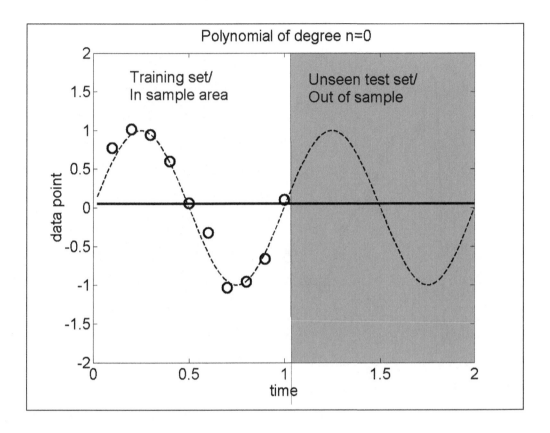

Figure 5.19: Predictive capability of the polynomial of degree = 9 for unseen test data. Curve generated with MATLAB.

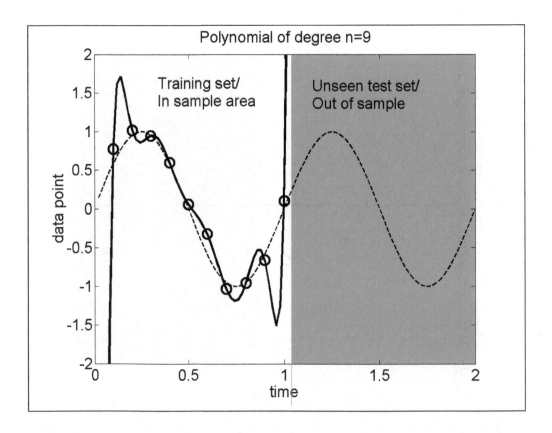

In contrast to this simple approximation of the training data set, let's have a look at the the polynomial of degree 9 (Figure 5.19). Obviously this complex polynomial (or trading system) does not have any predictive power for the future! The well curve fitted complex function misses the new points completely.

You might expect the best solution somewhere in between these two extremes. But this is not true. In fact no polynom of degree higher than 0 is a good approximation for the data points which are placed near a sine curve. All polynoms (even with degree 1) grow quickly away from the horizontal line around which the sine function oscillates. Thus all polynoms, except the polynom of degree 0, are useless concerning for making predictions! Although the polynom of degree 0 is poor it is the only robust one.

What is the way out of this situation? Does it mean that you must stop trading system development completely and look at the trend of the markets with simple lines?

Conclusions for trading system development

What you have seen in this example is just that markets cannot be approached with pure mathematical methods. But this does not mean that all trading systems must be of zero-complexity. Our mistake here was that we tried to approach a periodic sinus function with a non-periodic polynomial function. Like this we forced our algorithm to adapt to a situation for which it is not built. The polynomial function was not suited to the function we were trying to use it for because it is not the correct approximation for a periodic environment. The idea of periodicity was missing. The conclusion for you as a system developer and trader is that you must first have an idea of the market! Only when you have this can you start to code your idea and only like this will you get a code that makes sense. Just as it is useless to approach periodic functions with polynomials, it is useless to approach trendless markets with trend-following methods or to approach markets with no volatility with break-out systems. We know that this leads into further conflicts since markets are steadily changing, but using ideas and experience is the best approach you can take.

Further consequences of these tests are that once you have a simple, robust logic with a proper risk management in place you can stop your system development process. It is often better to use just one or two indicators, or only the price itself, rather than several combined indicators. Adding more and more rules will just increase the adaptation of your trading system to past market data, but it will not increase its predictive power for real trading. Therefore it is better to save your time and invest it otherwise, for example in adding a money management scheme or by diversifying your strategy with further simple but robust systems within a portfolio.

6

Periodic re-optimisation and walk forward analysis

6.1 Short repetition: "normal", static optimisation

Let's first remind ourselves of the "normal" optimisation process which we set out in Chapter 5. In order to optimise your system you take a fixed training data set ("in sample data") and then you apply the system to previously unseen data: this is the so called "test set" or "out-of-sample data" (Figure 6.1). In our example the training data set was about four years and four months, from 21/10/2002 to 28/2/2007 and the test set was one year and four months from 1/3/2007 to 4/7/2008.

Figure 6.1: Equity curve of system LUXOR for British pound/US dollar (FOREX) training and test period, 30 minute data. Training period 21/10/2002-28/2/2007 (white), test period 1/3/2007-4/7/2008 (green).

Obviously this well-known procedure of optimising your trading system on a special market has some disadvantages. You only have one in-sample and one out-of-sample area. The out-of-sample test range is usually the most recent data. The more data you have in the training set the more efficiently you can train your system to different market conditions (compare with Chapter 5.2). Further, keep in mind that this "normal" optimisation process can work well for sound trading systems for a certain time. But be aware that over a longer period of time the market structure could change. In such a case you will need to adapt the trading system as well. A purely static approach with the input parameters fixed forever will fail sooner or later. Since there is no system code which can work forever you have to change your system parameters from time to time. These are good reasons to look at more dynamic optimisation methods.

6.2 Anchored vs. rolling walk forward analysis (WFA)

If you take the above example but make the optimisation window bigger and bigger you arrive at an anchored WFA. The optimisation is anchored since it always starts at the same point of time (Figure 6.2A). This is the simplest form of WFA. It usually works best, like the static optimisation we examined above, when the tested market keeps its personality within the tested sample.

Figure 6.2A: Anchored walk forward analysis. For every new optimisation run the in-sample optimisation window starts at the same point of time but its length is subsequently increased. The unseen out-of-sample data follows.

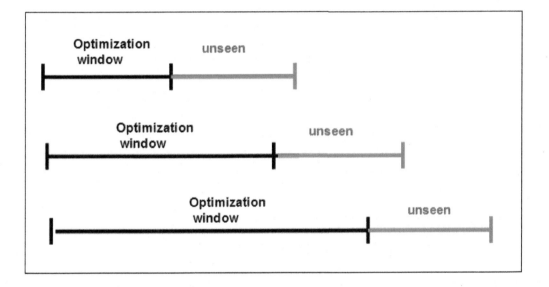

However, as you know, markets and their personalities can be complex. Sometimes a market will show an equity curve that has some very profitable and some not-very-profitable intervals within the tested data ranges. If a market appears to have such a changing personality then the anchored WFA may be not the best method. In these cases it is necessary to perform an optimisation method which better adapts to changing market conditions, the rolling WFA (Figure 6.2B). The rolling WFA is particularly appropriate for short-term intraday systems.

Figure 6.2B: Rolling walk forward analysis. Shifting in-sample optimisation window = 1 year and shifting unseen out-of-sample data = the 3 following months.

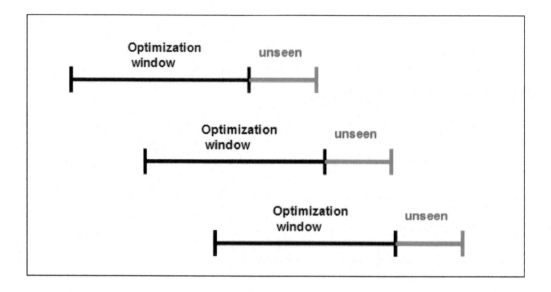

The better adaptation of the rolling WFA may mean it is more appropriate, and may yield results that walk forward better, in live trading than results obtained from an anchored WFA.

6.3 Rolling WFA on the LUXOR system

Periodic optimisation of the two main system parameters

Let's try the rolling WFA on the LUXOR system with 30 minute data of the pound/dollar pair. So instead of optimising the code's input settings within a fixed test data range, we now have to do a rolling re-optimisation of the two main system parameters, the fast and slow moving average. As seen in Chapter 5.4, the system is most reactive on these two moving averages that trigger the entry signals. During this re-optimisation process we keep all other system parameters (time filter and the three exits) constant with the values gained in Chapter 3. We optimise the two moving averages in periods of one year and shift this optimisation period three months further with every new run (Figure 6.2B). To complete the WFA and to check its results we apply the optimised values to the unseen data ranges. In this way we see how our periodically optimised system walks forward.

With the rolling WFA we have a training set which is not static as before but which is moving forward as the time goes by. In our case we use one-year in-sample optimisation periods which move forward every three months. With each new optimisation you get two new optimal moving average values. For example, during the optimisation period between November 2002 and November 2003 you get an optimal fast moving average length of 3 bars and an optimal slow moving average length of 21 bars. If you shift the optimisation period by 3 months to February 2003 until February 2004 the parameter's best values change to 1 (fast) and 39 (slow) for the moving averages. (Of course a "moving average" of length 1 is just the price itself.)

If you shift the optimisation window by 3 months again (now from May 2003 until May 2004) the two input parameters change again to 1 (fast) and 21 (slow) which is shown in (Table 6.1). So instead of the static optimisation you now have 19 optimisation runs for the two main input parameters within the training period. Please note that these 19 optimisation runs use nearly the whole market data range for both optimisation and for testing. Remember that the static optimisation from Chapter 5.4 just could use a small part of about one year of the data for the out-of-sample test. So you now get a much more detailed test of your trading system on much more data – not by having more data available (you still only have the 6 years from 2002 to 2008) but by using it in a cleverer way.

Table 6.1: Periodic re-optimisation of the trading system LUXOR on 30 minute data of the GBP/USD FOREX pair. The gained "best" parameters are applied subsequently to out-of-sample areas of 3-month test data.

Training Set				Test Set	
Training Start	Training End	Fast Moving Average	Slow Moving Average	Test Start	Test End
1-Nov-02	1-Nov-03	3	21	1-Nov-03	1-Feb-04
1-Feb-03	1-Feb-04	1	39	1-Feb-04	1-May-04
1-May-03	1-May-04	1	21	1-May-04	1-Aug-04
1-Aug-03	1-Aug-04	1	21	1-Aug-04	1-Nov-04
1-Nov-03	1-Nov-04	1	27	1-Nov-04	1-Feb-05
1-Feb-04	1-Feb-05	1	27	1-Feb-05	1-May-05
1-May-04	1-May-05	2	33	1-May-05	1-Aug-05
1-Aug-04	1-Aug-05	1	15	1-Aug-05	1-Nov-05
1-Nov-04	1-Nov-05	1	15	1-Nov-05	1-Feb-06
1-Feb-05	1-Feb-06	1	15	1-Feb-06	1-May-06
1-May-05	1-May-06	1	15	1-May-06	1-Aug-06
1-Aug-05	1-Aug-06	5	48	1-Aug-06	1-Nov-06
1-Nov-05	1-Nov-06	2	39	1-Nov-06	1-Feb-07
1-Feb-06	1-Feb-07	1	39	1-Feb-07	1-May-07
1-May-06	1-May-07	1	39	1-May-07	1-Aug-07
1-Aug-06	1-Aug-07	6	21	1-Aug-07	1-Nov-08
1-Nov-06	1-Nov-08	1	24	1-Nov-08	1-Feb-08
1-Feb-07	1-Feb-08	1	24	1-Feb-08	1-May-08
1-May-07	1-May-08	1	24	1-May-08	1-Aug-08

If you plot the two optimised input parameters as a function of the start of the optimisation window you see their change within the five years (Figure 6.3). Please note that the two optimised parameters change rather slowly – an important aspect for the gained out-of-sample test results, which we will discuss now.

Figure 6.3: Change of the optimal parameters for the fast and slow moving averages as a function of the shifting one year optimisation period. During the tests the following other parameters are kept in place: entry time window 9.30am-1.30pm GMT, exits: 0.3% risk stop, 0.8% trailing stop and 1.9% optimised for trading system LUXOR on 30 minute data of the GBP/USD FOREX pair.

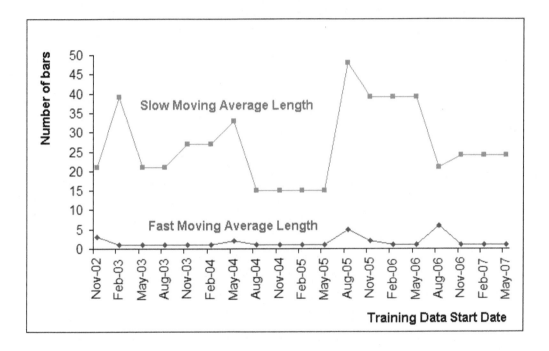

Out-of-sample test result

Let's apply the trading system with these optimised parameters to the unseen data. In Table 6.1 you can see that the optimal parameters 3 (fast) and 21 (slow) which have been gained in the first one-year optimisation window between 1 November 2002 and 1 November 2003 are applied to the subsequent three months from 1 November 2003 until 1 February 2004 of unseen data. The optimal parameters for the subsequent optimisation period (February 2003 until February 2004: fast moving average = 1 bar, slow moving average = 39 bars) are applied to the unseen data between 1 February 2004 and 1 May

2004 and so forth for all the other 17 periods. In this way you get a complete out-of-sample test of the trading system applied to previously unseen data. The result is shown in Figure 6.4.

Figure 6.4: Out-of-sample test for the periodically optimised values. System LUXOR for British pound/US dollar (FOREX) 2/11/2003-4/7/2008.
During the tests the following other parameters are kept in place: entry time window 9.30am-130pm GMT, exits: 0.3% risk stop, 0.8% trailing stop and 1.9% optimised for trading system LUXOR on 30 minute data of the GBP/USD FOREX pair.

The total net profit is slightly higher and the maximum drawdown lower than with the originally developed system. This is an astonishing result since this equity line is a 100% out-of-sample test for the two main input parameters, the fast and slow moving average. The explanation for this result can partially be given by Figure 6.3 and Table 6.1. There you can see that the two moving averages have had little need to change during the five years within the different optimisation windows. In other words the market conditions have not changed a lot and the system was fast enough to adapt to the changing market conditions which have lead to these profitable results.

Conclusion

The 30 minute data of the GBP/USD pair is a proper example of a periodic re-optimisation working with the chosen optimisation window (1 year) and shifting period (every three months). Please note, however, that the right selection of this re-optimisation window and period is a complex topic of which you should be aware. The periodic walk forward optimisation is one of the most powerful tools available today, but like every method it has its pitfalls and needs to be applied correctly. As with every optimisation the settings of an appropriate walk forward analysis depend on the number of variables in your trading system.

As we saw in Chapter 5, the less rules your system contains, the more robust your strategy will be in real trading. A trading system with too much complexity leads to too much adaptation of your system to the data and therefore to curve over-fitting. This rule, which was found in "normal" optimisation with one training data and one test data set can be transferred to the periodic re-optimisation. However, with the periodic re-optimisation you have the advantage that your out-of-sample data range (the test data) is bigger and therefore an over-fitted system with too much complexity usually fails in the walk forward analysis more often than it does during the static system tests. Because of this you can trust your system more when it passes the WFA than "normal" static back-tests.

6.4 The meaning of sample size and market structure

One point which is relevant during every optimisation process and especially of periodic re-optimisation is the question of how to choose your optimisation period. Do you re-optimise every day, every two weeks or every year? Your computer, with its limited power, may give an answer to this question but there are still other points there to investigate, one of which is the market's inherent attributes, which we call "market structure".

In our LUXOR system we had a rolling optimisation period of one year and a subsequent out-of-sample test period of three months. These chosen settings proved to be appropriate for our system/market combination. But what are good settings for other systems and markets? What if you work with daily data, with 10 minute data or with 1 minute data?

On a TradeStation forum we recently found a double-edged comment about this topic:

> The problem is that if you use an inadequate sample size then your system is much more likely to get "blindsided" by price patterns that haven't been previously observed when you implement it. Adequate sample size is the cheapest insurance a system trader can get. Unless a system is tested on an adequate sample of historical data, it is statistically impossible for it to walk forward reliably, no matter how good the test result looks. No amount of post-processing, analysis, walk-forward runs, out-of-sample testing or anything else can compensate for an inadequate historical data sample. If you sampled half a year of hourly wind speed data in Florida during a season when no hurricanes (or even any severe local thunderstorms) hit, you might come away with the impression that you had gathered a representative sample of Florida wind speeds.

Let's illustrate what this statement means. Figure 6.5 shows an artificial market as a function of time. As you can see our market is built in such a way that it has phases of slower and faster oscillations. In this case the structure of the market is a special oscillation or frequency. Of course markets can have hundreds of other typical attributes like opening gaps, trending behaviour, over-bought areas, etc. The fast and slow oscillation here is just a representation for a changing market structure.

Figure 6.5: The market changes as a function of the time. Every market has its special structure, frequency, trends etc.

Figure 6.6: Optimisation window fits to the market structure. Ideal case: unseen data is same as data in optimisation window.

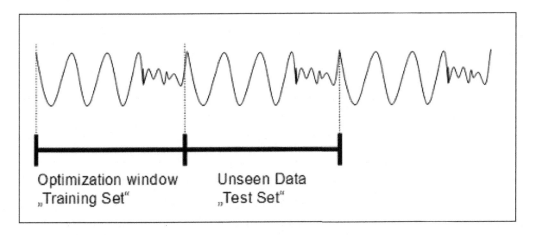

Optimization window
„Training Set"

Unseen Data
„Test Set"

Figure 6.7: Data in the optimisation window has a different structure than the unseen data. Worst case optimisation window.

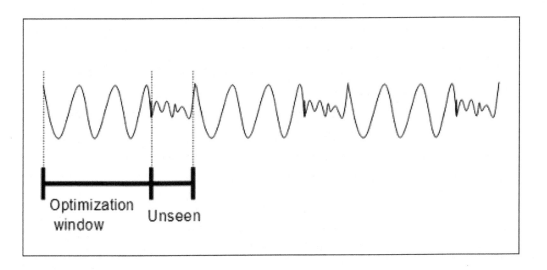

Optimization
window

Unseen

When you now apply your rolling WFA with shifting optimisation window and window of unseen out-of-sample data you can have the two extreme situations as shown in Figures 6.6 and 6.7. The optimisation window can catch a part of the market which contains all the information of the market (Figure 6.6) or it can be chosen in such a way that it just captures an area of market data which is completely different to the price structure which will follow (Figure 6.7). Obviously when doing WFA you will never have one situation or the other but always a mixture in between. What is ultimately suitable can only be discovered through a series of tests in order to gain the necessary experience of different scenarios.

Imagine that you run walk-forward tests on the S&P500, FTSE or DAX with different out-of-sample exclusion percentages and stress test coefficients on that same short sample of data, in order to get a quantitative idea of the number of walk-forward run and out-of-sample exclusion percentages that work best when walk-forward analysing your system. And let's also assume that you're unlucky enough that everything you run passes all the logical tests for reliability above the accepted threshold and comes out looking OK. Unlucky, you say? Sure, because you can slice and dice your data until your computer goes obsolete but you'll still never "see" the occasional market breakdown that occurs in the stock markets once in twenty years. That's because you're attempting to draw a set of complex statistical inferences out of a pathetically inadequate sample of data.

The longer your sample, the higher the probability that it contains most of the conditions it's likely to encounter in the future. It is human nature to want to curve fit a "beautiful" system to a short sample of data, but remember that sample sizing is a complex topic. There are high-risk but valid systems that trade very frequently, that may have a "shelf life" – the interval between re-optimisations – of a day or two and that might look at relatively short histories of data in n-tick or minute range timeframes. To a limited degree, data bars exhibit fractal properties. In other words, 20 years of daily data consists of about 5000 bars. A year of 15 minute cash session bars also consists of about 5000 bars. Both charts will exhibit similar patterns of trends, support and resistance, consolidations, double-bottoms, channel breakouts and other manifestations of the dynamic interaction of the group psychology of bulls and bears.

But does this mean that a year's worth of 15 minute data is equivalent to 20 years of daily data? No, it doesn't. The probability of recording a crash in six months' of data would not be any better if its sampling interval were three minutes instead of 60 minutes or daily bars. Be careful with short data samples regardless of timeframe or trading frequency. If your optimisation window is short, it is more likely you will miss important data outside of the window. You will be generalising on limited historical data, and this will lead to a weaker potential for predicting the future.

7

Position sizing example, using the LUXOR system

Steady money is not made by mysterious super trading systems, it is made by proper money management of average trading systems.

7.1 Definitions: money management vs. risk management

In order to understand what money management really means, its relation towards risk management is essential. Thus we first of all want to work out the different meanings of the two terms.

Risk management (RM)

Within a single trading system the simplest form of risk management is the control of the distance between the entry and the exit. As a practical example see in Chapter 3.5 how different stops and targets are added to an entry logic and how this changes the risk figures like maximum drawdown, average losing trade and largest losing trade. This step is the first in risk management and it is the implementation of the quantified risk values into your trading strategy. The second level of RM is the permanent measurement of risk during active trading. By screening your trading systems regularly, e.g. every month, you have to check if they continue to behave in reality as calculated during testing. You have to watch carefully if markets change concerning point value or volatility: this could affect your calculated risk figures and can mean that adjustments are necessary.

Money management (MM)

In simpler words MM is called "position sizing". It describes how to use your existing trading capital in the most efficient way and it provides answers to the following basic questions:

1.   What percentage of the available funds should be totally invested?

2.   What percentage of the available funds is it possible to risk in the next trade in a special market?

3.   What leverage and market exposure should be chosen?

The success of a trading strategy is highly dependent on correct money management. With appropriate money management techniques the existing capital should not only be maintained but increased in an optimal way. With prudent money management the loss of a single trade is limited in such a way that even if the trade goes wrong often, there is trading capital remaining to try many additional successive similar trades. All MM schemes have one thing in common: they only work on the basis of a trading system with a positive expectancy. Although a proper MM decreases the lot size in unfavourable phases it can only make gains if the system comes back and shows a profit factor higher than 1 in the long run. Whether the profit factor is 1.5 or 1.001 is not that important. As long as it is higher than 1 and the system makes steady profits a good MM can improve the results of your trading system. You do not need to have an extraordinarily profitable trading system to gain money. In the long term it's enough to have a stable strategy with a positive expectancy and proper money management.

From the above definitions of risk management and money management it is obvious that the two processes cannot be separated but they are highly dependent on each other (Figure 7.1).

Figure 7.1: The interaction of money and risk management. The goal of money management is to maximise your profits. The goal of risk management is to minimise your risks. The two different processes are connected with each other.

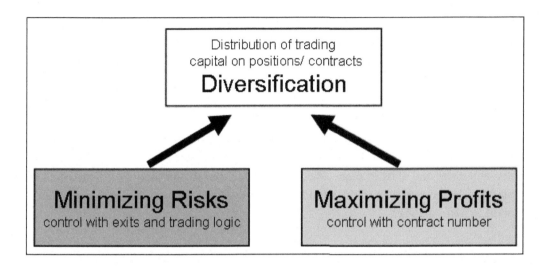

The distance of your initial stops and therefore the risk of your trading system is important for the determination of the number of lots you can trade. On the other hand the distribution of your trading capital is important in deciding how much you can risk in a single trade in a single market.

7.2 Application of different MM schemes

It is time to go from theory to reality and check how MM affects the results of our trading system LUXOR on the pound/dollar FOREX pair within the last 5 years. To keep things comparable we again work with 30 minute data. All computer tests in this chapter are calculated with $30 slippage and commissions per round turn.

You have probably heard about lots of different MM approaches like Kelly formula, Optimal F, Profit Risk Method, Martingale, Anti-Martingale etc. We do not want to indulge in an overview of all these methods with their pros and cons here. Instead we will choose only a few of them which we have found useful in our experience for real applications.

Reference: The system traded with one lot

Let's start with the result of the LUXOR trading system developed in Chapter 3, calculated with one fixed lot and a starting account equity of $100,000 (Figure 7.2). This equity curve is the simplest method of position sizing. It can be called "fixed size money management", which means in other words that you simply choose the number of shares or lots which are used for each trade. The main purpose of this approach is to provide a good baseline for comparison with more sophisticated money management methods which we will now expound.

Figure 7.2: Detailed equity curve. Traded with one fixed lot. Starting account size = $100,000. LUXOR system British pound/US dollar (FOREX), 30 minute bars, 21/10/2002-4/7/2008, with entry time filter and exits in place. Including $30 S+C per RT. An area with a recent small drawdown is encircled as a comparison for the following MM schemes. Chart created with Market System Analyzer.

Maximum drawdown MM

This method was used and described by Larry Williams [11]. The basic idea of this MM scheme is derived from risk management: you want to be sure you have enough equity in your account to withstand the worst-case drawdown the account has had in the past. At least, you would need enough equity to cover the size of the worst-case drawdown plus the margin requirement. This means that in order to trade one lot, you would need as a bottom line the one-lot margin requirement plus the worst-case one-lot drawdown. Larry Williams recommended, in order to make his MM a bit safer, to take 150% of the worst-case drawdown plus the margin for the first lot. Each subsequent lot is then added when the equity increases by 150% of the worst-case drawdown. This should ensure that you have enough equity to avoid losing everything even if the worst-case drawdown repeats itself. Let's see what this simple MM scheme does with our trading system (Figure 7.3).

Figure 7.3: 150% maximum drawdown MM by Larry Williams. Upper blue line: equity curve. Lower black area: number of traded lots. Starting account size = $100,000. Trend-following system British pound/US dollar (FOREX), 30 minute bars, 21/10/2002-4/7/2008, with entry time filter and exits in place. Including $30 S+C per RT. An area with a recent drawdown is encircled. Chart created with Market System Analyzer.

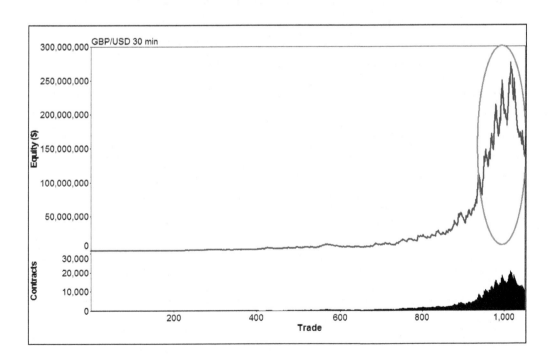

Instead of $120,000 profits without money management the system can now reach a final profit of $137 million with the applied MM scheme! But be careful. First of all the high number of 15,000 lots is not realistic. If you traded that much you certainly could not keep the same back-test result as with trading one lot. Even in the very liquid currency markets, such a high trading volume would change the market and lead to worse fills. Another point is the high risk of your trading system with the increased profits. Please note that the drawdown after the equity peak of $276 million is $139 million bigger than the left profit. So the higher gains have the price of higher risks. Let's see how other MM methods perform.

Fixed fractional MM

Fixed fractional MM was developed by another trader and book author, Ralph Vince, at around the same time as Larry Williams' maximum drawdown scheme [12]. Ralph Vince's method is also known as fixed risk position sizing because it risks the same percentage or fraction of the account equity on each trade. For example, with an account value of $10,000 a fixed fractional MM of 2% means that you want to risk a maximum of $200 per transaction.

But how do you set this risk of $200 in real trading? Let's check what this means with the example of our trading system and the pound/dollar. To answer this question we must go back to our previous findings, the strong interaction between risk and money management, and to Chapter 3 where we looked for exits.

We found an optimal stop loss value of 0.3% for the pound/dollar. With the pound/dollar trading at $2.00 the 0.3% stop loss would mean a risk of $600 for one lot (0.3% x $2.00 x 100,000) and this approach has not yet taken into account the slippage and the fact that even in the back-test the biggest loss was much bigger ($810). So obviously there is a dilemma. You cannot trade the pound/dollar currency pair with a $10,000 account equity with that 0.3% initial stop loss and a risk of 2%. The way out is to make changes to your money management or your risk management. You have to choose one of the following two possibilities:

1. Change of risk management: you set a tighter stop to lower your risk per trade.

2. Change of money management: you increase the account equity or you increase the risk.

There is a possibility that option 1 directly affects the trading logic. From all our findings about stops and profit targets we know that the trading system performance suffers with stops that are too tight. From the discussion in Chapter 3 you have seen that trades need enough room to develop. Tight stops remove this room and can turn a profitable strategy into a losing strategy. Since we do not want to change this risk management it means we must change our money management (possibility 2) and set the initial account value higher. Doing this is much easier to calculate but means in practice that you must have enough funds available. That's one reason why single traders very seldom use MM schemes and why bigger funds are more successful in the long run.

Let's calculate how much should be the minimum account. We want to risk 2% of our account with the next transaction. Since our risk with one lot is chosen by the preset stop loss of the trading system ($600), this means that the account must be at least $30,000, when trading one lot at this risk ($600 is 2% of $30,000). We take double this value to be sure not to conflict with our risk settings. So we trade one lot with $60,000. With a starting account value of $100,000 this means that one lot is allowed per transaction until the account value has reached $120,000 (= 2 x $60,000). The third lot can be traded when the account reaches $180,000 and so on. Please note that when the account equity decreases, the number of traded lots also has to be lowered accordingly. The result of this MM is shown in Figure 7.4A. You see that while the equity curve (blue line) is growing, more lots can be added (lower black area), until the highest account value of $790,000, reached in May 2008, when 14 lots are traded. When trading with so many lots the trading system comes into a drawdown phase (red encircled) which then leads to a bigger drawdown. Please note how this drawdown phase is huge compared with the original trading system traded with one fixed lot since now the drawdown is amplified by the 14 lots.

It is worth finding out what happens when we increase the risk per transaction more and more, to 5%, 10% then even to 30% (Figures 7.4B-D). As you can see the biggest equity point reached in May 2008 gets dramatically higher and higher. Whereas the fixed fractional MM with 2% risk reaches a biggest equity peak of $790,000, the MM with 5% risk reaches over $22 million, the MM with 10% reaches $981 million and the MM with 30% risk reaches over $6 billion!

But as you know, "trees do not grow to the sky" and the high profits have a high price. With the 30% fixed fractional MM finally "only" $538 million is left from the $6 billion reached before. So the suffered drawdown from the equity peak of over $6 billion was ten times higher than the final profit! The more aggressive the MM that is chosen, the higher the equity peak, but the bigger the drawdown which the equity curve suffers thereafter. The fixed fractional MM scheme works like an amplifier of the gains but also of the losses. You see again from this simple example, as with the above shown maximum drawdown MM, that although an aggressive MM seems to be attractive at the first glance because it promises big profits, the risks behind it quickly become too high.

Figure 7.4: Applying fixed fractional MM. The aggressiveness of the MM is increased from 2%, 5%, 10% up to 30%. Upper blue line: equity curve. Lower black area: number of traded lots. Starting account size = $100,000. Trend-following system British pound/US dollar (FOREX), 30 minute bars, 21/10/2002-4/7/2008, with entry time filter and exits in place. Including $30 S+C per RT. An area with a recent drawdown is encircled. Charts created with Market System Analyzer.

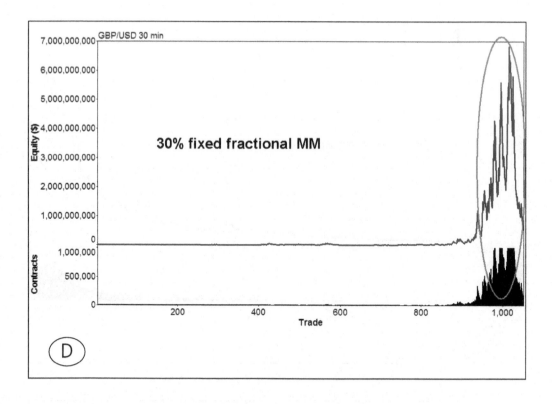

So let's see if there are more conservative methods out there.

Fixed ratio MM

Fixed ratio MM was first introduced by Ryan Jones in his book *The Trading Game* in 1999 [13]. In the fixed ratio position sizing the key parameter is the so called "delta". This delta is the dollar amount of profit per traded unit to increase the number of units by one. A delta of $10,000 means that if you're currently trading one lot you would need to increase your account equity by $10,000 to start trading two lots. Once you get to two lots, you would need an additional profit of $20,000 to start trading three lots. Then, trading with three lots, you would need an additional profit of $30,000 to start trading four lots and so on. The base to calculate the number of traded lots in fixed ratio position sizing is the following equation:

$$N = 0.5 * [((2 * N_0 - 1)^2 + 8 * P/delta)^{0.5} + 1]$$

N is the traded position size, N0 is the starting position size, P is the total closed trade profit, and delta is the parameter discussed above. As the mathematicians know $x^{0.5}$ means "square root of x".

A few points are worth mentioning. The profit P is the accumulated profit over all trades leading up to the one for which you want to calculate the number of lots. As a consequence the position size for the first trade is always N0 because you start with zero profits (P = 0). Please note that the account equity is not a factor in this equation, so changing the starting account size will not change the number of traded lots. Neither is the trade risk a factor in this equation – if trade risks are defined for the current sequence of trades, they will be ignored when fixed ratio position sizing is in effect. All that matters is the accumulated profit and the delta. The delta determines how quickly the lots are added or subtracted.

Ryan Jones' position sizing rule leads to a MM scheme which is a bit more conservative than the fixed fractional MM by Ralph Vince which was shown above. You can simply compare the two MM schemes as following (Figure 7.5):

Ralph Vince, fixed fractional lots = constant * account-size
Ryan Jones, fixed ratio lots = constant * squareroot(account-size)

So in contrast to the above situation with fixed fractional MM where the number of traded lots is linearly increased with the account size, with the fixed ratio MM the number of lots is increased like a square root function. This MM type is a bit more agressive in the beginning, but becomes more conservative and slower with more gained trading capital.

Figure 7.5: Fixed Ratio vs. Fixed Fractional MM. As trading capital increases, the fixed ratio MM increases the number of lots more slowly, with a square root function, than the fixed fractional MM, which works linearly.

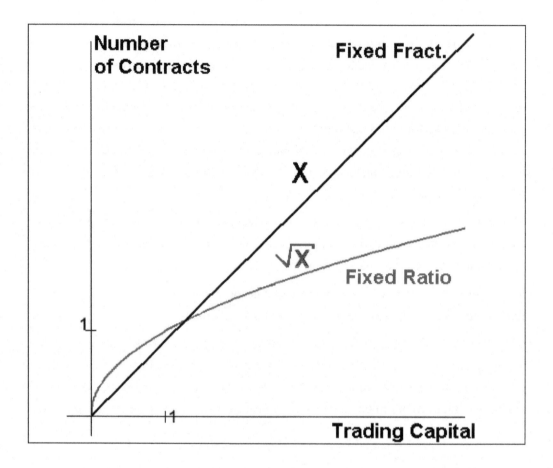

To see how fixed ratio MM works let's start with a delta of $100,000. This means that you can add the second lot only after your account value has increased by another $100,000 to $200,000 (Figure 7.6A). Obviously this MM is very slow and not much different from just trading one lot all the time so let's make it a bit more aggressive. (Figures 7.6B and C).

Figure 7.6: Applying fixed ratio MM. The aggressiveness of the MM is increased from A to C. Upper blue line: equity curve. Lower black area: number of traded lots. Starting account size = $100,000. LUXOR system on British pound/US dollar (FOREX), 30 minute bars, 21/10/2002-4/7/2008, with entry time filter and exits in place. Including $30 S+C per RT. An area with a recent drawdown is encircled. Chart created with Market System Analyzer.

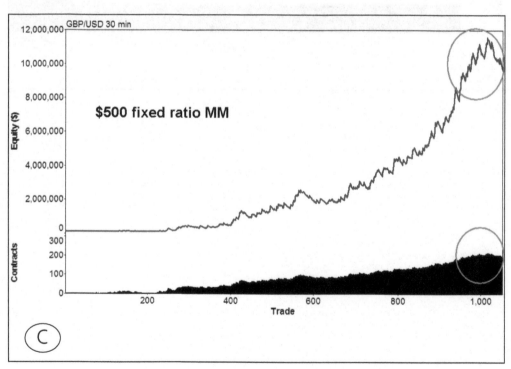

As with the fixed fractional MM the more aggressively you increase the lot size, the higher equity peaks you can reach, but also the bigger drawdowns you get in phases where the trading system shows some weakness. Compared with the fixed fractional MM the fixed ratio MM shows a better return/risk ratio as you can see when you have a closer look on the delta=$500 fixed ratio MM (Figure 7.6C). There you see that the equity high is $11.5 million and the drawdown is about $1.8 million. Although the drawdown is still excessive, the return/drawdown ratio is, with 6.4 in this example, better than the comparable 5% fixed fractional MM where you have an equity peak of $22 million but then a drawdown of $8 million leading to a return/drawdown ratio of 2.8.

7.3 Monte Carlo analysis of the position sized system

Position sizing increases your profits. But with the profits the risks also become higher. To get a better idea of how big the risks become we do a Monte Carlo analysis of the LUXOR system after position sizing and compare its results with the situation when no MM is applied (Table 7.1).

Table. 7.1: System figures without (green) and with money management (yellow). LUXOR system on British pound/US dollar (FOREX), 30 minute bars, 21/10/2002-4/7/2008, with entry time filter and exits in place. Including $30 S+C per RT.

	One Fixed Contract		$5000 Fixed Ratio MM	
Test period:	21/10/2002-4/7/2008		21/10/2002-4/7/2008	
Market	GBP/USD, 30 min bars		GBP/USD, 30 min bars	
Costs:	30$ Slipp. + Comm.		30$ Slipp. + Comm.	
Number of samples for Monte Carlo Analysis	5000		5000	
Max Number of Contracts	1		27	
Minimum Number of Contracts	1		1	
Average Number of Contracts	1		12	
Total Net Profit	**$132,590**		**$1,528,499**	
Starting Account value	$50,000		$50,000	
Final Account Equity	$182,590		$1,578,499	
Total Number of Trades	1,051		1,051	
Number of Winning Trades	370		370	
Number of Losing Trades	681		681	
Largest Winning Trade	$3,900		$90,144	
Average Winning Trade	$1,120		$13,737	
Largest Losing Trade	($810)		($15,418)	
Average Losing Trade	($414)		($4,860)	
Monte Carlo Analysis Results	**Worst Case Max. Drawdown**	**Worst Case Average Drawdown**	**Worst Case Max. Drawdown**	**Worst Case Average Drawdown**
ORIGINAL SYSTEM	($10,292)	($1,976)	($229,560)	($26,115)
MONTE CARLO RESULTS AT 90% CONFIDENCE	($16,136)	($2,176)	($295,316)	($29,168)
MONTE CARLO RESULTS AT 95% CONFIDENCE	($17,908)	($2,259)	($340,234)	($30,588)
MONTE CARLO RESULTS AT 99% CONFIDENCE	($21,364)	($2,308)	($446,064)	($33,182)

This table shows that the $5000 fixed ratio MM trades up to 27 lots simultaneously. This MM leads to a total net profit of over $1.5 million, compared to the $132,000 when trading one fixed lot. The price for the higher gain is higher risk. The MM increases the largest losing trade to $15,418 (from $810) and the maximum drawdown to $229,560 (from $10,292). The Monte Carlo analysis reveals that the worst case drawdown which can happen with 1% probability (since with 99% it is avoided) is now $446,064 (from $21,364).

7.4 Conclusion

The type of MM to select depends on the risks which you are prone to take. MM works like an amplifier of your trading logic, independently of which method you chose for position sizing. If it is properly adjusted then it will increase the profits of your trading system, but never forget that the risks are increased too – even with the best MM. In order to increase profits and at the same time keep the risk low it is advantageous to combine different systems and markets. You will find some ideas about this topic in the following chapter.

Part III:

Systematic Portfolio Trading

8

Dynamic portfolio construction

So far this book has shown methods to develop, test and evaluate single trading systems. This final section deals with the question of how to combine different trading systems and markets to construct a portfolio.

The topic is too large to provide a complete overview in this book, but in Chapter 8 and the appendix we have provided some practical tips from our own experience.

8.1 Introduction to portfolio construction

Even if many traders are aware of the notion that trading a portfolio of multiple systems on the same asset, or the same system on multiple assets, or both, smooths the overall equity line, few traders test and optimise a system with this perspective in mind. One motive for this in the past may have been that the most common technical analysis packages did not allow traders to produce a portfolio equity line easily. Nowadays things have changed and many software houses offer products that allow traders to test a multi-market multi-systems portfolio.

A list of the main available software

Market System Analyzer (www.adaptrade.com)

This is cheap and smart software that for as little as $349 can do whatever you need in the way of portfolio testing. It allows you to import system report data from TradeStation in Excel format, even if you need to do it for every single stock or future in the portfolio, (and this is quite time-demanding.) It performs equity line crossovers, Monte Carlo analysis, trade dependency and portfolio analysis.

MultiChart (www.tssupport.com)

This is a product that costs $1497 for a lifetime licence. It has a huge choice among different data feeds and it is Easy Language compatible. It can perform different optimisation and back-testing tests over a portfolio.

Mechanica (www.mechanicasoftware.com)

The former Trading Recipes has been updated and, after reshaping, has taken this new name. It has a standard edition that costs $3000 and a Professional Edition that costs $25,000. An upgrade from the old Trading Recipes costs $900.

RINA Systems (www.rinasystems.com)

This was the main portfolio software provider compatible with TradeStation for a long time. Portfolio Maestro (www.rinafinancial.com) is the flagship of Rina Systems and costs $10,000 per year. Portfolio Evaluator ($1295) is the first step in portfolio building for TradeStation users and in order to build a portfolio you simply need to shoot your system report into the Portfolio Evaluator platforms by pushing on the blue button in the TradeStation system report. Then you can build the portfolio by sticking together all the individual system reports. Portfolio Stream ($4995 individual purchase, $9995 professional purchase) does a lot more than Portfolio Evaluator, such as Monte Carlo analysis and walk forward analysis.

The role of correlations

Even though there are dozens of portfolio-building software programs available, the inclination to consider a single equity is still deeply rooted among traders. Nothing could be more wrong: with all the trading systems' intricacies set aside, a mediocre system optimised on a bunch of assets will be likely to produce a reasonable portfolio equity line. This should always be kept in mind when you scan different assets' prices with a newly-built trading system because what you are doing makes no sense if not included in a multi-market perspective. This is why we believe that approaching quantitative trading with a focus on a portfolio of assets, should they be stocks, futures, mutual funds or any other instrument, is a key element in surviving in the long run.

Today there is a deep flaw in the difference between what commonly-accepted financial theory predicates about portfolio construction, and what you can do with an average technical analysis software in practice.

Modern portfolio theory is built on the premise that in order to build an efficient portfolio you need to consider the correlations among the different assets. The more uncorrelated the assets the more efficient the portfolio, because if a position is losing, another position on a diverse asset will make money, dampening the overall effect on the portfolio equity line. The backbone of modern portfolio theory relies on the assumption that you cannot forecast the markets so that a systematic trader, who believes exactly the opposite, becomes confused on how to approach the topic.

Correlation is indeed a pivotal question for a systematic trader because if, for example, you are using the same system on different markets and this system is trend-following, it is clear in order to have two different positions – one losing and the other winning – you need to have some markets that trend and other markets that stay choppy (a situation that often occurs). But let's assume that you are trading multiple assets with two different systems, one trend-following and the other counter-trend. In this case you do not need all markets to be trending to have an upward sloping portfolio equity line. Some markets can trend and others can zig-zag with no definitive trend, and notwithstanding the overall portfolio will be profitable.

Let's move the reasoning a step ahead: let's assume that we have both trend-following systems (prone to exploit trending markets) and counter-trend systems (prone to exploit choppy markets) applied over the same markets. How does correlation fit into this picture? It seems that a sane reply would be simply that when it boils down to building a real portfolio with real trading systems the complex traditional theory totters and it shows how difficult it is to move from a pure theoretical world to the everyday life of a systematic trader.

Another critique of a portfolio approach based on correlation among assets is that correlation is not a stationary measure of the relative behaviour of two different assets. By stationary we mean that a form of correlation is not bound to last forever, economics change correlations among assets, so that presuming that in one year's time correlation will be the same as today could be fatal. Let's take the example of oil: economies were much more dependent on oil during the 1973-74 and 1979 shocks than during the 2008 bubble. So inflation perspectives during the 2008 bubble were much less imperative then 30 years earlier because Western economies were much less dependent on oil. The unfixed character of correlations is a controversial area that theoretical portfolio construction seems not to consider in an appropriate way.

Publications and theoretical tools

Among academic papers there is a shortage of good publications about portfolio construction with an algorithmic approach. One author that tried to fight against this situation is Thomas Stridsman. He wrote two inspiring books, *Trading Systems That Work* and *Trading Systems and Money Management*, where even without arriving at a final conclusion he tried to address all the relevant topics of portfolio construction properly. The rest of the technical literature on trading systems is almost silent on this approach. So, at this point it is impossible to go ahead with the sure support of an authoritative author and we need to navigate in uncharted waters.

Traders are often accused of being brutal and unfortunately we belong to this category. This is why our approach to portfolio construction is based on a practical approach that starts from a simple consideration: a trader, even a sophisticated one, should always be in control of what he does. We often meet professional traders, both private and institutional, that employ theoretical tools they do not fully understand or that they do not properly dominate. This is harmful when you come to real trading because markets are merciless. A trader, when using a trading system, needs to have total control of all its nuances. To employ complicated tools that require much time to be explored and understood is out of the reach of an average trader and portfolio manager. Time is short, markets are running all day long and you need to have a quick grasp of what to do without delving into complicated statistical problems.

Portfolio trading in practice

A sound approach to portfolio trading is something that is based on sound and prudent premises. Better, on sceptical premises. Scepticism in quantitative trading is the best rule you can apply since it lowers risk. It is hard to have doubts about everything but if you get accustomed to it you will arrive at the conclusion that there are just a few tenets that are really safe for a trader. We will now review some hard-earned lessons we have gained through experience:

The more the better

It would be unwise to dictate rules for the trading systems development field that should be abided only by traders who have huge programming and statistical skills or simply by professional traders that are backed by a powerful IT department. If you do not know how to make money in a discretionary way, every moderately good trading system (even a properly tested moving average crossover system) will be a better solution than merely following your gut feeling. Sometimes it can seem that to be a successful system trader you need to be a rocket scientist, though this is not the case at all. If you do not know how to make money in a discretionary way, whichever sound trading system you use will allow you to have an edge against the market.

It is useless to wonder if it is better to use a simple profitable moving average crossover system carefully optimised on a portfolio or a complex breakout and counter-trend system optimised with a detailed walk forward analysis if you are only able to have the first one. You can only trade with the tools and systems available to you and not with the tools and systems you would have in an ideal world. Time is money and sometimes it could be more rewarding to trade with a simple system rather than spending years developing a more complex system that is beyond your reach. A situation that often recurs in this business is the very sophisticated would-be trader that decade after decade keeps improving his system without ever applying it with real money, since it was not yet accomplished. Perfectionism is not a good quality in trading systems' development.

A price series is a price series and nothing more than a price series

A trading system should produce good results on a price series and not forcedly on a precise number of other price series. Thomas Stridsman argues that he usually tests a system over 30-60 markets along 20 years and he wants it to perform moderately well on at least two-thirds of all markets (see [1]). We think that this is a sophisticated approach and we agree with it, but we have encountered only a few trading systems that were successful on all markets. In many cases systems usually work with the same efficiency on futures that belong to the same category: bonds, currencies, stock indexes, cereals, etc. As stated above, there is not a clear recipe for success and you can only trade with the systems you have at your disposal today. If your systems work on all the markets you will trade on all the markets, but if they just work on three different markets they should not be discarded just for this reason.

We know what happened today but we have no means of knowing what will happen tomorrow

Cancel every "estimate" from your dictionary when you build a trading systems' portfolio. There are some authors that claim that you need to figure out your "estimated portfolio return and variance" in order to decide money management, systems and markets selection. This is the wrong approach because the very reason we are using trading systems is because we do not know how to predict the future and neither the expected average returns and variance can be estimated.

If we limit risks, profits will take care of themselves

We cannot control the profit of a position which we entered without the support of an estimate. What we control is the risk; that is the difference between the entry price and the stop loss. This is what we need to analyse in order to protect our capital.

This is a defensive approach to systematic portfolio trading and it must be clear that it does not exclude, once properly researched, other portfolio composition methodologies. As should be clear from the book, a trader should assess all the trading methodologies and tools the industry provides, but it is always prudent to apply only those methodologies that he can fully control and understand. The four points above are a kind of bottom line in systematic portfolio trading.

In the literature about trading systems there are really few ideas on how to compose a portfolio; that is, which markets to trade and which systems to apply to which markets. Usually in our business, where there is a lack of information about a specific topic it means that some gold nuggets are hidden somewhere. Portfolio composition is one such area that for years has not been able to overcome some useless ideas such as the Wilder's Commodity Selection Index or other more sophisticated approaches full of estimates, the origins of which nobody knows.

Let's look at some practical ways to build a systems portfolio. These approaches are real ones and have been applied either by us or by the best trading systems developers we have met in the last decade. We will not delve into the intricacies of each one because this would take us too far away from our path. Whichever method you decide upon, please test it carefully before trading. In this chapter we will pinpoint some hints about pros and cons you will encounter with every portfolio construction method.

Unfortunately we do not have a definite word about this subject: we believe that portfolio composition method can often depend on which systems you are adopting, and over all it will be affected by whether you are trading many markets with the same systems, many markets with many systems or one market with many systems.

Total vs. partial equity contribution

Once the system is tested against a basket of stocks and futures, and results are moderately positive on almost all the markets, the pivotal question will be whether to trade all the markets or to trade just those instruments where the system was best performing and discard the others. If you just follow this path, you will surely have the best historical equity line you ever saw, but you will probably go bust after a few trades. The common tenet here is that you need to trade all the markets because you do not know what will happen tomorrow. The futures that were the best performing could become choppy or the underperforming futures could become volatile and it may be easier to make money on them. Obviously there is no way for you to pretend you know which futures will be volatile tomorrow. Everybody would agree with this tenet. But before sticking to it without discrimination it is better we understand that it relies on some basic premises.

The first premise is that it assumes we just have a unique trend-following system or we just have a unique counter-trend system but not both of them. Only with one of these systems would we be worried if the market becomes respectively too choppy or too trendy. The second premise is that we need to apply the same system to all the same markets and not, for example, a counter-trend system to a traditionally choppy market and a trend-following system to a traditionally volatile market. If instead of having a single system to trade all the markets we have two different systems to trade all the markets this is surely a step ahead. We remind readers of our number 1 principle: the more the better. To arrive at a unique conclusion without specifying how many systems we have is impossible because we still need to make clear what the starting point is. If you just have a trend-following trading system it will be prudent to trade all the markets because you are not able to know in advance which market will trend and which market will be in congestion. If you have a trend-following system and a counter-trend system you can prudently trade all the markets or even apply the trend following system to the traditionally volatile markets and the counter trend to the traditionally choppy markets. This second solution is obviously more hazardous than the first but there are additional tools that can lower the risk.

Partial equity contribution

Another solution would be to test the systems on all the markets and then choose a fixed fraction of the best performing markets according to the broad category to which they belong: cereals, energies, currencies, stock indexes, bonds, etc. This portfolio is a kind of compromise between the total contribution and the all markets choice and it is neither too aggressive nor too defensive. This method could be the "golden middle".

8.2 Correlation among equity lines

As we have seen, this is one of the sacred topics of portfolio trading: look for those markets that are negatively correlated and trade them. In this way you can smooth the resulting portfolio equity line. The premise of this approach is always that you need to have the same system, set with the same inputs, on all the markets. If you trade a trend-following system and a counter-trend system the logic would require you to trade the same market in order to be sure that, whether it is trendy or choppy, you have a tool at your disposal that will fit the market situation and will make more money than the other one you trade. But there is a lot more in store for this approach. Nobody understands why you should check correlations on the price series instead of on the equity line itself. If you are a systematic trader you will not build your portfolio considering the price correlation among the assets, but you will only watch the equity lines and the correlations among them. If equity lines are growing it means that the systems are suitable to trade that market, if they are decreasing you would be better off to stop them.

Correlation among assets varies according to the economic situation. These changes take a lot of time to shape but once they take root they go ahead for years. So there is no reason not to exploit them. What we believe is that equity lines are the most suitable indicators for checking correlations among systems and among markets. More precisely when we quote equity lines, 'we want to measure the inter-correlations of daily equity changes among the different market systems' [12]. Price series themselves would be more important in terms of correlation if we were to manage assets using just fundamental analysis – their role in this case would be paramount in terms of asset allocation. It is not by accident that Portfolio Evaluator and Portfolio Maestro, the two flagship products of RINA Systems[6], use a correlation matrix based on monthly equity lines to calculate correlations among the different markets, and this is also the same for Market System Analyzer[7]. As far as we are concerned we would advocate the use of a shorter measure of correlation in order to minimise drawdown (weekly correlation or some form of averaging and smoothing of daily correlation). In our experience it is very difficult to find negative correlations among futures' monthly equity lines and even a negative correlation coefficient that amounts to -0.2 is really interesting in order to lower the portfolio drawdown (Figure 8.1).

Figure 8.1: Matrix of linear correlations among monthly equity lines of one of our portfolios traded with real money.

	BO	C	CL	FGBL	GC	JY	QM	SF	SM	TY	US	W	S	EC
BO		(0.2465)	0.0845	0.0971	(0.0162)	0.2678	0.2458	0.2354	0.1481	(0.0178)	0.0081	0.5000	0.4830	0.0962
C	(0.2465)		(0.0218)	(0.0334)	0.0944	(0.1478)	(0.1656)	0.1085	0.0349	0.1350	0.1129	0.0315	0.4600	0.0082
CL	0.0845	(0.0218)		0.0502	(0.0024)	0.1159	0.5514	0.1630	0.0755	(0.0019)	0.0158	0.0920	(0.0345)	0.0691
FGBL	0.0971	(0.0334)	0.0502		(0.1612)	(0.0187)	0.1421	0.2673	0.1600	0.3054	0.1733	0.0439	(0.0551)	0.0000
GC	(0.0162)	0.0944	(0.0024)	(0.1612)		(0.0351)	0.0462	0.0285	0.1195	(0.0360)	(0.0838)	0.0437	0.1981	0.2711
JY	0.2678	(0.1478)	0.1159	(0.0187)	(0.0351)		0.1819	(0.0304)	0.0971	(0.1208)	(0.0050)	0.2806	0.2511	0.1176
QM	0.2458	(0.1656)	0.5514	0.1421	0.0462	0.1819		0.2274	0.1419	(0.0835)	(0.1079)	0.1026	0.0669	0.1926
SF	0.2354	0.1085	0.1630	0.2673	0.0285	(0.0304)	0.2274		0.0704	0.0075	0.0089	0.1198	0.2008	0.1664
SM	0.1481	0.0349	0.0755	0.1600	0.1195	0.0971	0.1419	0.0704		(0.0880)	0.0172	0.0498	0.2007	0.2108
TY	(0.0178)	0.1350	(0.0019)	0.3054	(0.0360)	(0.1208)	(0.0835)	0.0075	(0.0880)		0.3063	0.0197	0.0159	(0.2185)
US	0.0081	0.1129	0.0158	0.1733	(0.0838)	(0.0050)	(0.1079)	0.0089	0.0172	0.3063		0.0841	0.0363	0.0100
W	0.5000	0.0315	0.0920	0.0439	0.0437	0.2806	0.1026	0.1198	0.0498	0.0197	0.0841		0.4674	0.0616
S	0.4830	0.4600	(0.0345)	(0.0551)	0.1981	0.2511	0.0669	0.2008	0.2007	0.0159	0.0363	0.4674		0.2080
EC	0.0962	0.0082	0.0691	0.0000	0.2711	0.1176	0.1926	0.1664	0.2108	(0.2185)	0.0100	0.0616	0.2080	

---

[6] See www.rinafinancial.com
[7] See www.adaptrade.com

As you can see there is no negative correlation lower than -0.30. By the way, this is a portfolio multimarket multisystem dating to May 2008. The average starting period is 2001-2002 when electronic markets were launched, but many trading systems – on FGBL (German Bund Futures) for example – are much older. The more uncorrelated asset seems to be the 10 years Treasury Bill (TY) which has a negative correlation with at least 7 other equity lines out of 14 (50% of the markets). The second most uncorrelated are GC (Gold) and JY (Japanese Yen). The most correlated asset is Wheat which has no negative correlation with any other. In second place, Eurodollar (EC), Swiss Franc (SF) and Soybean Meal (SM) have a negative correlation just one market out of 14.

The most common way to compose a portfolio with a matrix of correlation among equity lines is to attach more weight to those price series that are uncorrelated with the others in order to smooth the portfolio equity line. In the example of Figure 8.1 Eurodollar, Swiss Franc and Soybean Meal would be the price series with the lowest number of contracts to be traded while Gold and Treasury Bills should be weighed more than any other asset.

8.3 A dynamic approach: equity line crossover

Every trader is haunted by the obsession of the possible failure of the systems he is trading. This is the psychological burden systematic traders need to withstand in order to achieve success. A common way to gauge a system's failure is drawdown or a multiple of the drawdown. We believe that, even if the drawdown figure is important, it is not the key element in evaluating the performances of a trading system. If you do not pretend that subsequent trades are dependent on preceding ones, drawdown is just one of the possible sequences of losing trades a system can encounter. Moreover, drawdown is the direct misfortune a trader can encounter in his job, not something that he could enjoy, and it would be inappropriate to use drawdown, or even worse a multiple of it, as a final threshold before stopping a system.

So the idea is why not use a dynamic approach that indicates to the trader when the system starts faltering? And over all why not adopt a general objective approach that indicates not only which systems are stopped because they are out of synchronisation with the market but also which ones to activate because they start to be in synchronisation with the market? What we would like is to set criteria for discarding a system when it starts to lose money but also criteria for activating a dormant system when it fits the current market conditions. So the idea is to trade a system when the equity line crosses over the 15-30 period moving average of the equity line itself and stop trading with a system when the opposite is true (Figure 8.2). The same crossover rule could also be applied to the whole portfolio of systems as a second security measure after being applied to the single system. In this case it would be proper to distinguish between a portfolio of daily systems (it would not be advisable to exit a trade on a daily trading system simply because the portfolio equity line dropped below its average) and a portfolio of intraday trading systems.

In our experience it is not a sure thing that this equity line crossover approach will work equally well on all systems and all markets. If the system is a good one, if it does not have too many rules and if it is properly optimised and equally properly re-optimised at periodic intervals, it is likely that the equity line crossover approach will never encounter a downward crossover. So if the system is too good, applying this approach will never improve the overall system results. However, applying the equity line crossover to the whole portfolio of systems with a whole portfolio equity line is a tool that can help the trader prevent the nightmare of the "black swan" when everything goes wrong.

Usually the equity line crossover is a dynamic tool that reduces the risk more effectively than the use of the simple drawdown. Moreover, the simple drawdown rule or a multiple of it has no corresponding contrary rule to activate a "dormant" system, whereas our proposed security rule can give this indication.

Figure 8.2: The blue line is the 30-period moving average and the red line is the 1-period equity line. At point A there was a down crossover and trading was stopped. At point B there was an upward crossover and trading was resumed.

8.4 Dynamic portfolio composition: the walk forward analysis activator

This is a brand new approach. It was developed by Fabrizio Bocca and Cristiano Raco, two brilliant Italian systematic traders, and has not been disclosed so far. Let's look at an example on an intraday trading system which is put under periodic optimisation every 3-months inside a process of walk forward analysis. If during the 3 month periodic re-optimisation the system has a walk forward efficiency ratio of more than 50% then it is traded in real time and conversely if the walk forward efficiency ratio goes under 50% then the system is momentarily stopped. In this way we can decide which trading systems in our trading systems' farm are to be applied and which ones are to be suspended. Fabrizio Bocca classifies all his systems in relation to the walk forward ratio every 3 months and then he allocates his trading capital to those systems that have the highest rank.

Figure 8.3: this is an example on how Fabrizio Bocca and Cristiano Raco rank their trading systems' farm though WFA. On the right corner there is a column denominated RCD where the WFA results are condensed in a comprehensive index. If the index is positive the trading system is traded with real money, if it is negative (zero in the column) is it deactivated.

N.	Trading System	MM	P16 Months	PI 12 Months	MI 13 Years	PI Years	RCD
1	Euro Rev Br	15	0,183	8,443	12,729	10,422	9,314
2.	Open Week Bund	30	1,338	2,054	10,262	17,404	8,300
3.	Bund Kagi Daily	30	6,039	1,826	7,837	11,500	6,797
4.	Gold Kagi Daily	30/15	-1,000	2,069	6,349	11,016	5,110
5.	Euro Nightmare	15	5,951	4,314	4,135	7,210	5,067
6.	Bund Big Deep	30	4,193	6,540	3,477	2,690	4,193
7.	Dax Castle	15	0,235	1,237	3,832	9,649	3,807
8.	TBond DBZ	30	1,754	1,918	4,918	4,510	3,612
9.	Mazzle Dax	15	2,983	3,871	2,564	4,044	3,250
10.	TBond Kagi Daily	15/30	3,954	1,682	2,525	5,966	3,217
11.	Crude Oil Multi	30	0,387	-0,477	2,013	3,318	1,407
12.	Fib Castle	15	-1,000	-0,034	1,122	4,302	1,151
13.	Big Deep US						0,000
14.	Vit Daily Bond US						0,000
15.	Open Week Dax						0,000
16.	Open Week Spmib						0,000

8.5 Largest losing trade/largest losing streak/largest drawdown

Another way to compose a portfolio of different markets and systems would be to normalise risk by the largest losing trade or drawdown. This is one of the most popular approaches. In this way the system with the highest losing trade, largest losing streak or largest losing drawdown will have the lowest number of contracts allotted to it and conversely the system with the smallest losing trade, losing streak or losing drawdown will have the highest number of contracts allotted. Obviously the loss figures on which this method is based make sense only if you do not consider WFA, otherwise these loss figures will vary with every WFA you periodically make. Moreover if you adopt this approach with largest losing streak or largest losing drawdown then you must believe that trade dependency has some value since otherwise it would be difficult to believe that the trade sequence will repeat itself in the future exactly as it did in the past. If the trade sequence varies drawdown will also vary. As for the use of the largest losing trade, you need to consider that a theoretical test will never encompass mistakes and slippages and in our experience these are the best candidates to be the largest losing trades. In any case, the largest losing trade, being precisely just one trade, has a low statistical significance but many traders use it because it is easy to grasp and apply. We have nothing against it, but – as with everything – it should be regarded with caution and the drawbacks it entails should be kept in mind.

Conclusion

The trading system's code: is this the pivotal issue in quantitative trading? We believe that programming is just one of the many factors involved in trading systems development. The proof of this statement comes from experience on the field: in 15 years we have seen many successful systematic traders but in only a few instances were they professional programmers. So where was the edge? We believe the edge was in understanding how and when to apply a system and understanding when to stop it. No system is forever. Markets change, traders change, systems change. Nothing is everlasting. Success is easy to reach with a code and a limited period, but really rare over 10 or 20 years. So if you think that systematic trading is a job for life please do not overrate the importance of programming skill.

Let's make a comparison with a lawyer: is the knowledge of law important for a lawyer? Of course it is. But also social relations, character and the family background are equally important. If you are a lawyer and you know the law perfectly, but you run your business in a little town, you will seldom become involved with a nationwide criminal case that will project you into the stratosphere. If your social environment is comprised of little shop-keepers and retired persons you will care about minor civil suits. If you play golf in New York with famous bankers and financial directors it is likely that you will care more about high-profile cases. The same applies with trading system development: it is important to have some basic programming capability but if you want to be successful a lot of other skills are required such as networking with other systematic traders, following publications and seminars on the topic, purchasing and trying new software and attending scientific meetings and the conferences of professional organisations, like those of I.F.T.A (International Federation of Technical Analysis).

Now we know what you think: if your ideas are disclosed to a programmer then he will make money with them. But there are many points against this idea. The first is that if your programmer makes money with your ideas this will not prevent you from making money with them all the same. We have already discussed that you can publish your system in the *Wall Street Journal* and people will not trade it. So do not be scared about giving away some "secrets", provided these are really such as you presume they are. Second, it is very rare that a programmer will have the time, the feeling or the capability to understand if a code is really important. Programming and testing are two different jobs. It often happens that testing is not done in a systematic way. All traders believe they have a feeling with some particular markets and timeframes and there are few traders that test a system over 70 markets and 10 timeframes. So even if the programmer has the intention to steal something it may be that he will not grasp what he is really stealing. To test a system over many markets and timeframes, to understand if something is missing, how to cure its shortcomings and how to improve its efficiency is something that is a big job on its own, far away from the programming skill.

The best systems we developed were fixed by professional programmers that we are sure did not understand what they were programming. Then a last consideration: if you come up with two ideas per day and your programmer puts them into a code at the end of the year there will be so many ideas and codes that he will bored and he will never check anything more from you. Testing and fine-tuning a code is a really time consuming job, and very expensive also because you need to have many data sources and many data providers in order to easily cover all the markets and all the timeframes.

A good systematic trader does not have a single code but dozens of viable trading systems' codes that he selects and applies according to the current market conditions. So a really good systematic trader will never refuse to exchange cards with you. If you have 40 systems and you exchange some systems (it is better not to exchange the best performing systems on sensible timeframes, e.g. 1-3 minutes), with some other systems you will end up with more systems and no harm to your systems farm. A mediocre systematic trader has just one or two systems and he thinks that their codes will bring him success, so he keeps them in a safe and he would prefer to die rather than give them away.

The more complex the system the more easily it will be over-optimised with too many variables or inputs. If you are not a sophisticated programmer this could be good luck because you will never run the risk of writing codes that are too lengthy.

Another point comes to mind when you are considering our professional activity in the last 15 years from a historical point of view: codes and ideas are almost the same, there is nothing really conceptually new in trading systems. You have tons of opening range breakout codes, pivot points, channel breakouts, etc. The same stories are oft-repeated but still work intermittently in today's markets. You can find thousands of these formulas for free on the internet with little effort. You can even know that Jim Simons, the best quant trader around, who made a huge personal fortune with his Magellan Fund, is trading mostly with Markov chains and on an intraday basis. Would this be enough for you to emulate his success? No, it can help you in going in a precise direction but it will never allow you to have any practical tips on the feeling, the approach and the theory that lies in his trading systems. So the key point is not the code, the key point is how to adapt existing codes to the current market conditions, how to build a portfolio and how to know when the moment comes to stop a system and start another one.

But let's add another point which is more human than strictly technical. Like in many other human endeavours, persistence and determination are those qualities that sooner or later lead to success. The programming capability, the mathematical background, the creativity are all factors that surely help in algorithmic trading, but the most important thing will be the feeling you have with the markets, the trades and the systems. And this feeling is the relentless result of persistence and determination. To gauge systems, to develop systems, to evaluate quantitative trades it takes years. It could not be possible in any other way: success is always difficult to reach and for a systematic trader success is money.

The thread that occurred to us during this book is very clear: do not think that a powerful trading platform can transform you into a successful trader, do not think that one piece of code instead of another will bring you to success. It will take a lot of hard work and a little bit of chance.

This is why we did not merely write down our receipt for success, we did not fill the book with codes, and we did not use complex concepts to explain the simple steps for successful systematic trading. We recommend that you are always in control of what you do: do not listen to the sirens that pretend you will make money with their complicated software, their academic seminars and their 1000-page books. Be flexible, cynical and scared: a systematic trader is always sitting on the bomb that will sooner or later explode and kill him. As Thomas Stridsman put it, probabilities are that we all will go bust sooner or later. If you start from this point, chances are that you will survive a long time.

Every methodology we highlighted in this book alone will not be the ultimate key for a profitable systematic trading but all put together they will paint a clearer picture in which you can move comfortably just owning a simple trading system's code.

Let's review all the methodologies and try to summarise the pros and cons of each of them.

Rule complexity

It is better to trade with a system with few inputs, few variables and an equity line that is not historically exhilarating instead of 100 inputs or variables and a super equity line.

Testing

Do not put your focus on a bunch of markets and forget the other ones. Nobody could tell you that a system does not perform on a market but could be the winning tool for trading the remaining 50 markets. Subscribe to a data vendor such as CSI data (www.csidata.com) or Pinnacle data (www.pinnacledata.com) and then apply your systems on at least 70 different futures daily price series before arriving at the conclusion that the code does not work.

Optimisation

Optimisation is good if it is performed in a savvy way. You should re-optimise regularly, after a fixed time period in order to keep the system in synchronisation with the market.

Monte Carlo analysis

This is a good process in order to check the stability of the system in a probabilistic way but its importance should not be over-stressed. If the systems is over-optimised the Monte Carlo analysis will be perfect but this does not mean anything.

Portfolio building

If you are trading an easy code like a channel breakout, or a moving average on a bunch of portfolios to choose the right prices series to be traded, this is a vital point for success. We depicted many ways to approach this problem, but the final solution will depend more on the experience of the trader than on a precise rule.

Dynamic risk management

Do not rely on a fixed rule in order to activate or stop a system from trading. You need to run a farm of a dozen trading systems and then activate those that are fit for the current trading environment. The moving average equity line crossover is this kind of tool that can transform a mediocre system into a powerful trading machine.

Money management

This is one of the most important factors in trading, always keep your risk exposure less than 1% from the entry point per every trade, better to be 0.5% is you are able to afford such a low risk level.

As you can see from the above mentioned points, the systematic trader has at his disposal a long list of tools that can overcome the would-be higher efficacy of the programming complexity without hurting the profit attractiveness of a trading system. And we stress that you should pay heed to this list in order to improve results.

Appendices

Systems and ideas

In these appendices we have included three trading systems. We explained the first two in articles in *Traders* magazine and the third one was extensively treated within this book. These three systems can be used as a starting point to build portfolios with trading systems.

Appendix 1: Bollinger Band system

1.1 Idea

In this book we already used a Bollinger Band system to show the effect of out-of-sample deterioration (Chapter 5.2). The Bollinger Band which we use now to build a simple, but robust portfolio, was described in detail in an earlier article in *Traders* magazine [14]. Its trading logic is explained with Figure A1.1.

The first third of the graph (August to October 2004) shows a phase of lower market activity. The volatility drops and the Bollinger Bands become narrower. During this period of lower volatility the market often tends sideways without any direction. Many market participants are unsure about the further development and stay on the sidelines.

Such phases of decreasing interest of market participants form the base of succeeding considerable movements. The longer the indecisive phase is the stronger is the subsequent breakout (see Figure A1.1, mid-October until December 2004). After the breakout the Bollinger Bands widen and follow the trending price very quickly. From Figure A1.1 you can calculate the profit of the trade which uses this impulsive long breakout. It brings 6 cents (=7500 US dollars in the euro future) although some of the gains have been given away. Shortly after the long exit a short signal was triggered (February 2005) which turned out to be a false breakout and was soon exited by the moving average stop.

1.2 Entry logic and Easy Language code

Long entry:

If the price crosses above the higher Bollinger Band. Enter the market intraday with a buy stop:

Enter long: next bar at HigherBand stop;

Short entry:

The short entry is symmetrical to the long entry, enter intraday if the price crosses below the lower Bollinger Band.

Enter short: next bar at LowerBand stop;

Exit:

Exit if the price crosses the moving average between the Bollinger Bands:

Exit: next bar at Average(Close,60) stop;

The exact position of the higher and the lower Bollinger Band is determined by taking the simple moving average and adding (higher band) or subtracting (lower band) the following, volatility dependent amount: Distance * Standard deviation. The volatility dependent component is located within the standard deviation, whereas the distance is a fixed parameter which can be varied.

The Easy Language Code is just some lines:

```
Inputs: Length(60), Distance(2);
Vars: HigherBand(0),LowerBand(0);


HigherBand = Average(Close, Length) + Distance * StdDev(Close, Length);
LowerBand = Average(Close, Length) - Distance * StdDev(Close, Length);


Buy next bar at HigherBand stop;
Sell next bar at LowerBand stop;


ExitLong next bar at Average(Close, Length) stop;
ExitShort next bar at Average(Close, Length) stop;
```

The system has two input parameters, which are bold typed. One represents the length of the moving average, the other determines the distance (or width) of how far away from this moving average the Bollinger Bands are placed. Their default values are set to a length of 60 and distance of 2. By changing these parameters you can adjust the trade frequency. The smaller you set the length for the moving average, and the smaller you choose the distance of the Bollinger Bands, the faster the system will react to market changes and the more signals you will get. As well as this possibility to adjust the system code to your personal needs Bollinger Bands have further advantages for building mechanical trading systems. Due to their volatility-based component they can easily adapt to different market conditions. Additionally they provide a natural exit point by using the moving average between the Bollinger Bands.

1.3 Application of the strategy to seven markets with same parameters

The strategy is now applied to daily data of seven markets from three different market groups:

Three stock index futures:

Nasdaq-MINI, EURO STOXX 50 and Swiss Market Index

Two bond index futures:

Bund, US-T-Note (10year)

Two currency futures:

Euro and Swiss Franc

Daily data was taken from mid-1994 until mid-2005. Data source for the end-of-day data was CSI Unfair Advantage (csidata.com).

For all the performed tests exactly the same parameters (default: length=60, distance=2) were taken in order to minimise the effect of curve fitting. All results are based on a one contract per market basis and are presented without subtraction of slippage and commissions.

1.4 Results and conclusions

The combined equity line of the seven markets looks like a good starting point for a viable trading system (Figure A1.2). For more detailed information have a look at the system figures (Table A1.1). You can take this system and combine it with other uncorrelated systems/markets within a bigger portfolio.

As mentioned, the system was not optimised concerning the input parameters for the entries. More important to note, however, is that we have not inserted and optimised any special exits into the system. If you do this in the way it was shown in Chapter 3.5 of this book, results can be improved, especially concerning risks and drawdowns.

Figure A1.1: Euro in US dollar, daily, with Bollinger Bands and 60-day moving average of closing prices. The entry and exit points are marked with circles. The crossing of the price and the Bollinger Bands generate the long and short entries. The crossing of the price and the moving average triggers the exits. Chart created with TradeStation 2000i.

Figure A1.2: Combined equity line of the Bollinger Band system for the portfolio of seven markets, 08/1994-09/2005, for daily data. The figure shows the added net profit on a bar-by-bar basis of all trades on these markets without slippage and commissions. Chart created with RINA Systems.

Table A1.1: Key figures of the system tests based on end-of-day data. The second table below shows the main figures of the Bollinger Band system for the portfolio of seven markets, 08/1994-09/2005, applied to daily data. The table shows the added results of all trades on these markets without slippage and commissions.

Bollinger Band System	
Seven market portfolio	
System Analysis	
Net profit	$220,943.00
Gross profit	$451,455.50
Gross loss	($230,512.50)
percent profitable trades	42.15%
Avg. Win/ avg loss.	2.69
profit factor	1.96
maximum drawdown	($8,120.00)
average drawdown	($1,424.51)
number of trades	261
average trade	$846.52

Time Analysis (Days)	
percent in the market	82.28%
longest period out (days)	77.00
Average time in market	59.53
average time between trades	2.14
average time in winning trades	103.71
average time in losing trades	27.34
average time to reach new high	120.10

Appendix 2: The triangle system

'The symmetric triangle is one of the most profitable patterns for short-term trading.' [15]

2.1 Idea

Figure A2.1 shows a chart of the continuous, back-adjusted euro/dollar future contract (Globex) at the end of January 2007. You see that within three days a very nice, symmetrical triangle developed. The triangle pattern is a very strong, profitable pattern since the logic behind it is sound.

It uses a similar idea to the Bollinger system presented in Appendix A1. The triangle system is more exact in its entry however. Again, as with the Bollinger system, a phase of uncertainty leads at first to a compression in the market. The volatility decreases while the triangle pattern gets narrower. And again like in the Bollinger system, this phase of decreasing interest of the market participants is the reason for the succeeding movement. The longer the indecisive phase lasts, the stronger the subsequent breakout is. At a certain point, when the consolidation has continued for a longer time while many market participants are unsure about the further development, any distortion, e.g. a news event, can create a strong breakout. Many traders which had been standing on the sidelines before are now in a hurry to jump onto the driving train, and like this they amplify the emerging trend. This is underlined by the increasing volume when the breakout happens.

2.2 Programming and coding

Please note that we do not disclose this code but just describe its logic.

But, as you might have recognised, before that final breakout occurred smaller movements out of the boundaries of the triangular figure took place. While a good discretionary trader might ignore the false breakouts, such "spikes" are difficult to program on a computer. First of all it is difficult to identify such a triangular pattern. Then if your algorithm has found it, to draw the legs of the triangle you must tell the PC where the triangle starts and which points define the legs. Will you ignore the spikes in your calculations or will you include them? This will be different for each situation. Furthermore when will the triangle end and how will you calculate the profit target from the triangular shape? For the discretionary trader these points are very easy to see, but on a PC it is a long list of programming tasks.

To overcome these issues we took a different, more abstract approach. We add a simple moving average of the last 200 closing prices and a volatility indicator of the last 300 bars to the same euro, 5 minute chart (Figure A2.2). On this example you see how the symmetrical triangle can be programmed. The figure shows that shortly before the breakout occurred, at the position of the black vertical line (called "set-up point"), two conditions were true at the same time:

1.   The volatility indicator of the last 300 bars has dropped to its lowest point.

2.   The moving average of the last 200 closing prices is moving nearly horizontal.

With these two clear simple conditions we can program the set-up of the triangle pattern, or better call it the low volatility/flat moving average pattern. Because like this we do not program a pattern recognition logic which is identifying symmetrical triangles. Instead we are only looking for low volatility phases and for phases in which the market tends sideways at the same time, described by the horizontal movement of the moving average. This is a much weaker condition than the exact pattern recognition but helps us to simplify our programmed trading system logic to put it into reality. Our two set-up conditions could well occur in other patterns, e.g. if the market consolidates within a rectangular small trading range.

Now the entry logic can be completed as following. If our set-up with the two conditions is true we place a long entry stop order a fixed amount above the current market price and symmetrically a short entry stop order the same amount below the current market price. The long and short entry levels act as a natural stop loss and reversal point of our initiated positions. So if we have entered the market long and the market shortly after proves us wrong and changes to the down side, we exit our long position and enter the market in the opposite direction short. Thus our logic lets the market decide about its breakout direction and just follows it. We exit the position at a profit target which we determine from the difference of the high and the low within the last 300 bars (see yellow vertical lines in Figure A2.2). If the profit target is not reached shortly after the breakout we exit the position with a trailing stop instead.

2.3 Application to different liquid futures markets with same parameters

We apply our gained system code to 5 minute data of four different markets from different liquid futures markets groups: the euro/dollar future as a currency market, the S&P 400 MidCap future as a stock index, the US-T-Bond-Future as a bond market and Light Crude Oil as a liquid commodity future. As data supplier we took the intraday data feed of TradeStation 8. We tested our system within the period of the last five years on back-adjusted futures data from January 2002-January 2007 on all four markets with same system parameters. Our computer simulation is calculated with $30 slippage and commissions per round turn ($30 S&C per RT).

The equity curves all grow very steadily with only minor drawdowns (Figures A2.3a-d). The best equity line seems to be Light Crude Oil. Also very steady over the tested five years were S&P 400 MidCap and US T-Bond Future. On the other side the euro future had a sideway phase for the last two years with its biggest drawdown happening just recently, in January 2007 (-$4,575). Overall the equity line, which you get by adding all trades, is however still clearly positive. If you watch the equity curves of the single markets more closely you see that they look a bit like stairs. The reasons for this behaviour are long lasting, flat periods between the signals. The system is only about 1-2% of the total time in the market, the rest of the time it is flat.

It is an important characteristic of our system that signals occur very seldom, but when trades are taken they tend to result in big profits.

2.4 Advantages in building a portfolio

A very positive side effect of the system's low market exposure is a very low correlation of the system's results when applied to the four different markets simultaneously (Table A2.1). You can see that the correlations of all four systems' results are nearly 0, they vary between a very small negative correlation of -0.002 and a small positive coefficient of 0.024. This practically uncorrelated behaviour of the four markets helps to build a high return/low risk portfolio when combining them. You can also see that while the maximum equity drawdowns of the four single markets vary between -$2,440 (S&P400 MidCap) and -$4,590 (US Treasury Bond Future) the maximum equity drawdown of the four-market portfolio is in the same area with -$3,275. So while the profit of the portfolio grows in a linear way with the added markets to over $58,000, the maximum drawdown is kept in the area of one single market. This results in a very steady portfolio equity curve (Figure A2.4). It is worth mentioning that even within the four-market portfolio the system is only in the market for 10% of the time. So the market exposure is very low, which would allow you to add further systems or markets to the portfolio.

The trade statistics reveal that the gains of the system don't come from a high winning percentage (53%), but from the fact that the average winning trade is a huge amount bigger (factor 1.4) than the average losing trade. Furthermore, the average time in trades is very small, at 0.3 days. This shows that the system captures mainly dynamic breakouts which happen very fast and only last for a short time.

The system figures reveal a further quality of the triangle system: the equal weight of long and short trades. From the total 625 trades long and shorts nearly have the same number (322 vs. 303) and the profits are nearly divided equally between the long and short side. This applies for the single markets and as well for the combined portfolio. This feature is the result of the construction of the trading logic, which lets the market itself decide in which direction it goes and just follows it, with the same probability in the long and in the short direction.

2.5 Conclusion

The example of the triangular pattern clearly shows the different tasks of discretionary and systematic traders. While discretionary traders can rely on their experiences and their ability to estimate the market correctly, systematic traders need to act in a different way. As many patterns which are easy visible with the human eye cannot be programmed directly, we took a different approach and simulated the pattern with common indicators: a moving average, the volatility and the price itself. With this approach we could not exactly simulate the triangular pattern but we created a trading system which comes close to the conditions which are true within such a triangle pattern: decreasing volatility and sideways market direction. Like this our trading logic was gained by pure market observation and not by optimisation or curve fitting. We are rewarded with a very robust system which stays profitable over different markets with the same input parameters. At the first glance it seems to be a disadvantage that signals occur very rarely and that the time in the market is very low, but it is this fact which makes different markets completely uncorrelated for our trading logic and allows us to build a profitable low risk portfolio.

Figure A2.1: Principle of the symmetrical triangle pattern, discretionary view. Euro, Globex, 5 Minute, 21-24 January 2007. A natural profit target can be derived from the width of the triangle. False breakouts usually occur which make triangles difficult to program for systematic trading. The final breakout takes place with volume increase and leads the price into the target region.

Figure A2.2: Principle of programmed triangle system. At the point before the breakout occurs (set-up point) the volatility is extremely low and the moving average tends sideways. If these two conditions are true, a long stop and a short stop entry order is placed. These entry levels also work as natural initial stop and reverse points. A profit target is derived from recent highs and lows (yellow lines).

Figures A2.3a-d: Result of triangle system on four different markets: 6/2/2002-6/2/2007, $30 S&C per RT, on a day-to-day basis.

A2.3a: Euro/dollar Future (TradeStation symbol @EC)

A2.3b: S&P 400 MidCap Future (TradeStation symbol @EMD.D)

A2.3c: US T-Bond Future (TradeStation symbol @US.P)

A2.3d: Light Crude Oil Future (TradeStation symbol @CL.C)

Equity curve detailed – @CL.C 5 min(02/06/02 00:10 – 02/06/07 13:35

3 d) Light Crude Oil

Figure A2.4: Equity curve of 4-market portfolio. Triangle system applied with same system parameters to the following markets: euro/dollar Future, S&P400 MidCap Future, US T-Bond Future and Light Crude Oil Future. Equally weighted on a one-contract basis, including $30 S&C per RT, Jan 2002-Jan 2007, calculated on a day-to-day basis. Chart created with RINA Systems.

Detailed equity curve – 0 (01/21/2002 – 1/19/2007)

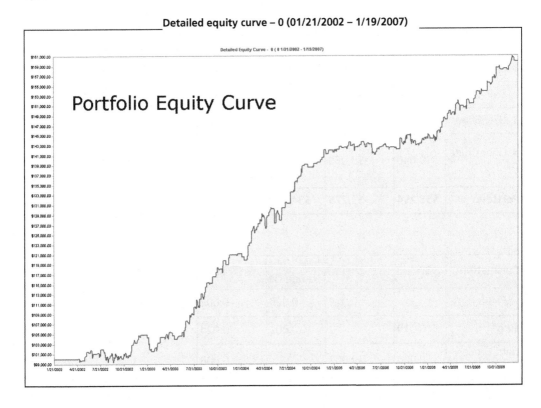

Table A2.1: Portfolio figures, Jan 2002-Jan 2007. Portfolio figures of Triangle system applied to the following markets: Euro/dollar Future, S&P400 MidCap future, US T-Bond-Future and Light Crude Oil Future. Same system parameters for all markets, $30 S&C per RT, calculated on a day-to-day basis.

Market	Net Profit	Max. Drawdown	Net Profit Long	Net Profit Short	Number of Trades	Average Trade	Percent Profitable
1. Euro	$15,915	-$4,575	$8,693	$7,222	197	$81	49%
2. S&P 400	$11,280	-$2,440	$6,810	$4,470	149	$76	54%
3. US-T-Bond	$12,019	-$4,590	$9,556	$2,463	140	$86	57%
4. Light Crude Oil	$19,040	-$3,050	$9,570	$9,470	139	$137	53%
Portfolio	$58,254	-$3,275	$34,629	$23,625	625	$93	53%

Correlations	S&P 400	Euro	Light Crude Oil	US-T-Bond
S&P 400		0.019	0.020	-0.002
Euro	0.019		-0.002	0.024
Light Crude Oil	0.020	-0.002		0.006
US-T-Bond	-0.002	0.024	0.006	

Appendix 3: Portfolios with the LUXOR trading system

In Chapter 3 we presented the trend-following system called LUXOR and tested it extensively on the British pound/US dollar pair.

Now we are going to check this trading logic on other markets. We will outline how this strategy works on various bond markets and how to use it to construct robust portfolios.[8]

3.1 Idea

Before trying to code an idea with the purpose of building a systematic trading methodology it is important to understand the inner nature of the different markets you are going to trade. The market most appreciated by traders is the equity indexes universe. Stocks, that are the components of the equity indexes, move more following psychology than real events. Just think how an event could impact a stock: it is always an indirect influence, very seldom a direct one. Oil prices are going up? An oil stock can benefit from this situation but it will benefit more or less depending on its corporate efficiency, from the relative competitive position in the industry, from the intelligence of its management, and so on. Surely it will benefit but how much it will benefit is always a matter of discussion. But if we are talking about oil, the true commodity, the real black gold, this is another story.

---

[8] More information about this topic can be found in [16].

Commodity prices are influenced by real demand and real offer. Psychology is still important but not dominant. If China is growing 10% per year in the following 10 years, the demand of all kinds of commodities will perhaps double or triple, nobody knows for sure. This is a direct effect: Chinese importers are bidding for oil on the international cash markets and prices are going up. Nothing is more easy to understand. This is why psychology will be more important on stocks than on commodities.

But there will be another aspect to consider also. If we are talking about "indirect effects", it means that there will be few events that everybody will agree will modify the picture of the equity indexes. On the equity indexes everything is smoothed by discussion, interpretation, indirect effects, and so on. When, on the contrary, news directly affects demands and offers, and the news is dramatic, there is no room for discussion and interpretation. Prices jump or they crash. *Tertium non datur.* So you will have limit up and limit down days, you will have huge price swings in one direction or another. But in this black and white world, in between psychology and real demand and offer, you have a third environment: bonds.

Monetary policy has a steady nature, no climax, no sudden changes. Economic swings are slow and seldom do they surprise markets. In a period of economic recession interest rates will go down for months after months, in a period of economic expansion interest rates will go up smoothly. Take for example the 17 interest rate increases in the US: at a certain point the market discounted them and it was obvious that they would then have to go up once again. A misunderstanding could only really have occurred if you were at the very beginning of the 17 interest rate increases or at the end of them. Please note, though, that we are talking about two situations out of 17.

In a more serious way we can say that elements of a macroeconomic series are quite auto-correlated, so that if they start rising they will go on for a while, if they will go down they will go continue down for a while. Monetary policy is not a kind of situation where one day you have an increase of 2% and tomorrow a decrease of 3% and then tomorrow again an increase of 1% and so on. This is why prices in bonds tend to follow the same direction without much noise and this is why moving averages on bonds are a good predictive tool, because they are simply able to catch this smoothing behaviour of prices. You should have no fear in trading bonds with moving averages. From all our performed quantitative tests and experience we can conclude: they work!

3.2 The trading logic

You can find all the details on the logic of the LUXOR system in Chapter 3 of this book, so we won't discuss it further here, but will focus on the results of the strategy.

Please note that we do not apply any additional exits to the strategy at this point. Trades are only exited when the price crosses the slower moving average of the entry logic (in case of long positions). The system is built symmetrically concerning long and short trades.

Of course you can and should add exits which meet your personal needs to the strategy. You will find the appropriate methods on how to adjust them in Chapter 3.5 of this book.

3.3 Results in the bond markets

Let's see how the LUXOR system works on the major bond markets. We want to check if bond markets really fit well with trend-following systems as we expected from our fundamental argumentation above.

All the following tests are based on a one-contract basis and are performed with the following input parameters of the system (fast moving average length=7, slow moving average length=26). No adaptation of the parameters to the different markets was performed in order to keep the results comparable and to avoid the effect of curve fitting.

The strategy is applied to the daily data which was provided by CSI Unfair Advantage (csidata.com). The futures data was point-based back-adjusted to get rid of artificial gaps between different contract months. All results in the figures and tables are based on a one contract per market basis.

If you apply the LUXOR system to the bond markets, you see that in all of them you get more or less steady equity curves (Figure A3.1). Some work better, like the US T-Bond, the US T-Note (10 years) and the German Bund, and some look a little bit worse, like the not so well known Australian 10-year Treasury Bond or the Korean 3-year Government Bond. But with all of them you get positive results.

In order to add the results of all tested bond markets to a combined portfolio, you have different possibilities. You could first convert the point values and currency of each market and build a portfolio in US dollars. For this you must convert the Korean bond, Japanese bond etc, by using the dollar conversion rates $/won, $/yen etc and then add all equity-lines. To simplify these calculations we used another method here. We tested all the single bond markets in points. We made a simplification to add these point equity curves of all 12 markets to get a portfolio. This is not 100% mathematically correct but the result comes very close to what it would be if you were to use the exact currency conversion rates (for example 1 point in the Bund future is 1000 euro, 1 point in the US T-Bond and US T-Note is $1000 and so on).

The equity line becomes very nice and steady, you only get minor draw downs (Figure A3.2). The most significant one happened in 1994 during the bond market crash, when all markets turned their trend from upside to downside more or less at the same time. But on the combined, long-term equity line it looks more like a small accident than a big issue.

If you have the capability you could trade this portfolio in the three different time zones with all included markets. There is, however, one reason why we won't advise you to do this, even if the equity line looks good enough: correlation! All the bond markets are so highly correlated that the possibility exists that the system might crash for all the markets at the same time, as happened partially in the year 1994 – just imagine if you were long in all 12 bond-markets and then they all go down at the same time. The high correlation increases the risk of your bond portfolio drastically.

In order to build a high return/low risk portfolio, the concept should be as follows: take a mixture of different systems and apply them to different markets in different timeframes. For example you could choose some liquid markets from the bond group and apply a medium-term trend-following system, like the one described here. Then you would add, for example, swing-trading systems for the currencies and day-trading systems for the Mini S&P and so on. Various possibilities exist which you must fit to your personality and your trading style. The whole topic is too big to treat it seriously here.

3.4 Diversification with other market groups

Here, to stay with our trend-following logic and to get a better feeling for it, we build a small portfolio of different market groups.

We use two bond markets, the German Bund and the US T-Note (10 year) but add other markets from different market groups: the euro/dollar as a currency, the Mini S&P as a stock index plus Gold and Light Crude oil as famous commodities. So we have a portfolio in which the successful bond markets still build the core but which is diversified with less correlated markets. It is important to mention here that the Mini S&P produces a negative equity line, the Gold goes just sideways and the euro/dollar weakened in the last 3 years as well (the equity lines are not shown here).

Even with these markets included the overall portfolio shows a steady upward equity line, since the two bond markets and the crude oil kept the portfolio running well. The equity line does not look as steady as for the complete bond portfolio, but that's what we expected.

The idea here is to have a portfolio of less correlated markets in which there are always one or two that have big gains that compensate the losses of other markets.

Let's have a look at the portfolio's main figures (Table A3.1). The system figures which we get are typical for a trend-following system. Only 37% of all the 3168 performed have been profitable. The overall big gains of the system result from the high ratio of average win/average losing trade which is nearly 2.5. A very important fact to mention is the following: the system's gains resulted from the 63 positive outlier trades. These outliers produced more profit ($606.487) than the final total net profit ($526.259)! This means that the extreme big winning trades made the profit of the system. This underlines again how important it is in trend-following systems to let the profits run. If you missed the positive outliers you would have no gain at all. The annoying point for you as a trader is, however, that such big gains occur very seldom, but when they do occur, you must catch them.

An interesting fact of the system is also that the average time in winning trades is more than four times longer than the average time which the system stays in losing trades (25 days versus 6 days). This shows again how the trend-following logic cuts the losses short and lets the profits run.

3.5 Conclusion

With the examples presented above we wanted to show you how important it is for successful trading to select the right systems for the right markets. With the bonds we have identified a group which could have been exploited perfectly with trend-following methods lasting recent decades. From the fundamental point of view the chances are good that they will continue to behave like this. We are aware that a trend-following system is not suited for every trader. It's annoying to have only a small amount of profitable trades and to wait most of the time until the big moves take place but trend-following strategies work too well in bond markets to not use them. They are a key part in the most successful existing hedge funds. In our opinion they should be at least one component of your trading systems if you want to be successful in the long run.

Figure A3.1: Equity Lines of 12 major bond markets, in points. Conversion from point values to base currency: German Bund: 1 point = 1000 euro; US T-Bond, US T-Note (10 year) and US T-Note (5 year): 1 point = $1000; US T-Note (2 year): 1 point = $2000; Eurodollar (3 month) 1 point = $2500; Long Gilts: 1 point = £1000; Canadian Government Bond (10 year): 1 point = C$1000; Canadian Bankers Acceptance (3 month): 1 point = C$2500; Japanese Government Bond (10 year): 1 point = 10000 yen; Australian Bond (10 year): 1 point = AU$1000; Korean Government Bond (3 year): 1 point = 1 million. Korean won. End of test period in all markets: April 2006. Charts created with TradeStation 2000i.

Figure A3.2: Portfolio of 12 combined bond-markets. The system equities in points of the following markets were summarised: German Bund, Long Gilt, US T-Bond (30 year, electronic), US T-Note (10 year, electronic), US-T-Note (5 year, electronic), US-T-Note (2 year, electronic), Eurodollar (3 month, electronic), Canadian Government Bond (10 year), Canadian Bankers Acceptance (3 month), Australian 10 year Bond, Japanese Government Bond (10 year), Korean Government Bond (3 year). August 1977-April 2006. Chart created with RINA Systems.

Figure A3.3: Portfolio of 2 bond markets and 4 markets of different groups: German Bund, US T-Note (10 year), Mini S&P, Gold, Light Crude Oil, euro/dollar. $30 slippage and commissions per trade subtracted. May 1972-April 2006. Chart created with RINA Systems.

Table A3.1: System figures for the 6-market portfolio consisting of German Bund, US T-Note (10 year), Mini S&P, Gold, Light Crude Oil, euro/dollar. May 1972-April 2006. All numbers are calculated with $30 slippage and commissions per trade.

System Analysis			
Net Profit	$526,259.20		
Gross Profit	$1,620,546.45		
Gross Loss	($1,094,287.25)	Total Slippage & Commission	$95,040.00
Percent profitable	37.59%	Profit factor	1.48
Ratio avg. win/avg. loss	2.46		
Annual Rate of Return	1.90%	Sharpe Ratio	0.92
Return on Initial Capital	87.71%		
Return on Max. Drawdown	1337.42%		

Total Trade Analysis		
Number of total trades	3,168	
Average trade	$166.12	
Outlier Trades	Total Trades	Profit/Loss
Positive outliers	63	$606,487.35
Negative outliers	4	($24,871.00)
Total outliers	67	$581,616.35

Time Analysis	
Percent in the market	86.51%
Longest flat period	24
Avg. time in trades	12.95
Avg. time between trades	0.48
Avg. time in winning trades	24.92
Avg. time between winning trades	2.27
Avg. time in losing trades	5.74
Avg. time between losing trades	2.67

Equity Curve Analysis	
Avg. time between peaks (days)	73.32
Maximum Equity Drawdown (daily)	($39,348.75)
Date of Maximum Drawdown	13/12/2000

Bibliography

[1]   Stridsman, Thomas, *Trading Systems That Work* (McGraw-Hill Professional, 2000).

[2]   Aronson, David, *Evidence-Based Technical Analysis* (Wiley, 2006).

[3]   You, Dr. Alex, http://elsmar.com/pdf_files/Degrees_of_Freedom.pdf

[4]   Pardo, Robert, Design, *Testing and Optimization of Trading Systems* (Wiley, 1992).

[5]   Jaekle & Tomasini, "Channel Breakout – Part 4: Light Crude Oil", *Traders* (2008).

[6]   Stridsman, Thomas, *Trading Systems and Money Management* (Wiley, 2003).

[7]   Collins, Art, *Market Beaters* (Traders Press, 2004).

[8]   Jaekle & Tomasini, "The importance of time for short-term trading", *Traders* (November 2006).

[9]   Sweeney, John, *Maximum Adverse Excursion: Analyzing Price Fluctuations for Trading Management* (Wiley, 1997).

[10]   Farrell, Christopher, 'Monte Carlo models simulate all kinds of scenarios', *BusinessWeek* (2001).

[11]   Williams, Larry, *The Definitive Guide to Futures Trading, Volume II* (Brown Co, 1990).

[12]   Vince, Ralph, *Portfolio Management Formulas: Mathematical Trading Methods for the Futures, Options and Stock Markets* (Wiley, 1990).

[13]   Jones, Ryan, *The Trading Game: Playing by the Numbers to Make Millions* (Wiley, 1999).

[14]   Jaekle & Tomasini, "Bollinger Band System", *Traders* (2006).

[15]   Jaekle & Tomasini, "The Triangle System", *Traders* (2007).

[16]   Jaekle & Tomasini, "Trend following in the bond markets, Part 1 and 2", *Traders* (2006).

Index

A

account size 165-6, 169

Active Trader (magazine) 9

algorithmic trading 3-4, 9, 192, 195

Aronson, David 111, 115, 121

automated trading 3-4

average time in trades 31-2, 46, 207, 225

B

back-test 15, 46, 50, 60, 108, 155

black swan xii, 189

Bocca, Fabrizio 190-1

Bollinger Band system 115-120, 201-7

C

code 145, 221

    Bollinger Band system 117, 203

    constituent parts of 41

    example 4

    importance of 111, 193-5

    LUXOR 39-40

    optimising 19, 148, 150

commission (see: trading costs)

complexity (see: polynomial curve fitting and trading systems, complexity)

cost of trading (see: trading costs)

currency market, attractions of 37

curve fitting 20, 108, 144-5, 158, 204, 213, 223 (see also: over-optimisation)

"cut losses short" 46, 225

D

degrees of freedom (df) 15-18, 24, 115, 127, 155

    definition 16

determined (approach to trading) 195

discretionary trader(s) 5-6, 9, 183, 210, 212

E

Easy Language 10, 39-40, 41, 202-3

equity line crossover 180, 188-190

exits (see also: stop loss(es))

    and money management 83-6

    determining appropriate 64-86

F

fixed fractional money management (see: money management, fixed fractional)

FOREX, daily volume 59

fundamental analysis 10, 187

future(s) 10, 13-14, 121, 185, 196, 204, 211, 223

Futures (magazine) 9

N

net profit/maximum drawdown ratio (NP/DD) 71, 74, 75

O

optimisation 19-24, 26, 49-59, 79, 90, 115, 118-9, 126-135, 147-158, 196

    definition 19

    improving equity lines and 131-3

out-of-sample

    data 90, 147, 149-150

    deterioration 121-2, 129, 135

    period 21, 22

    test 23, 100, 126, 148, 151, 153, 156, 157, 159

over-optimisation 23, 108, 194, 196 (see also: curve fitting)

P

persistence 195

polynomial curve fitting 136-144

portfolio(s)

    building 3, 5, 31, 179-192, 180-2, 184, 185, 197, 212-3, 224

        equity line crossover 180, 188-190

        walk forward analysis activator 190-1

    construction (see: portfolio(s), building)

    correlation and 181-182

    management 3

    trading 183

position sizing 162, 164, 168-9

profit target 76-84

psychology, behind the markets 29, 158, 221-2

Q

quantitative

    finance 4-5

    methods 4

    technical analysis 8

    traders 5

    trading 5, 181, 183, 193, 195

"quants" 4

R

Raco, Cristiano 190-1

retail traders 5, 11

RINA Systems 32-3, 52, 54-6, 180

risk management (RM) 3, 5, 10-11, 64-86, 87, 145, 159, 161, 164, 197

RM (see: risk management)

rule complexity 15-16, 134-5, 136, 142, 196

S

sample size 29, 155-6, 158

selection without replacement 103, 108

short market bias (see: market data, bias)

slippage (see: trading costs)

software 3-4, 87, 90, 179-180, 181

    list of available 180

    technical analysis 5

    TradeStation 8 90

CPSIA information can be obtained
at www.ICGtesting.com
Printed in the USA
BVOW10s1623130716

455452BV00004B/11/P